Praise for Clean Language

And What Happens Next …? Forged from the brilliant and original ideas of David Grove, Wendy Sullivan and Judy Rees bring their own professional experiences to offer the reader thought provoking and invaluable information to challenge everyday beliefs, thoughts and decisions made in business and personal development.

Cei Davies Linn, Former wife and partner of David Grove

So, in the world of Clean there's going to be a change, a BIG change. A Clean Change! At the turn of the millennium, Penny and James with *Metaphors in Mind* led us to the font of Clean. Now, in 2008 Wendy Sullivan and Judy Rees have given us the cup to drink from it! This book is guaran-teed to become THE place to start with Clean Language. I know that with this resource at hand, attendees at training courses and clients around the world will have at their fingertipsthe essentials to become effective and proficientin the theory and application of Clean Language. Starting out with the basics and through simple, 'easy to swallow' activities the reader learns and experiences the nuances of this powerful technique. And as they continue to drink the depth and level of understanding consumed through the pages of this book, they *will* have learnt how to facilitate themselves and others in changing their lives.I would like to congratulate Wendy and Judy on a great piece of work! WELL DONE!

Matthew Hudson, Clean Language and Emergent Knowledge facilitator, former assistant to David Grove, www.powersofsix.com

Clean Language is one of the most fundamental and important tools available in NLP and coaching. This book stands out for the clarity of its explanations and makes Clean Language commonsense. This book is to be used as the communicators bible.

Toby McCartney, WestOne Training, Author of *Mastering Memory*

This book promises to transform the way we think about language and meaning. After reading Clean Language, the words and metaphor that seemed so throwaway yesterday become a vitally empowering tool for today, and tomorrow.

Psychologies Magazine

In their excellent book, *Clean Language: Revealing Metaphors and Opening Minds*, Wendy Sullivan and Judy Rees give an in-depth yet highly accessible route-map for understanding the metaphorical nature of human perception, and for developing powerful skills for working in the domain of personal metaphor.

While I expected the subject to be covered in masterful detail, what I didn't anticipate was such a cogent and useful introduction to the role metaphors play in perception. Wendy and Judy present this material in a way that's easy to grasp, and pull together understandings and realisations that you would otherwise have to piece together from diverse sources.

Of course, the core of the book is the application of the Clean Language questions. There are numerous exercises for developing intuitions about what to ask when, and for what purpose. If you've been wondering about what "Clean" is and how you can use it, or you've already got some skills in this powerful domain, Wendy and Judy's book will provide you with new depths of insight, skill and effectiveness.

Jamie Smart, Licensed NLP Trainer, CEO of Salad

With this book, Clean Language comes of age. From the clear definition in Chapter 1, through the many transcripts of Clean conversations and activity exercises driving the learning home, to the informative case histories and appendices at the end, this book romps along in an easy to read style that keeps you turning the pages. By the time you get to the meaty technical stuff in Chapter 5, you are thoroughly hooked and ready to pay the attention required. Practitioners such as therapists, psychologists and coaches will glean a clear understanding of why asking people to create their own metaphors works better than leading them through guided visualisation scenarios, and how to do it. For business managers, the great learning will be that Clean Language proves invaluable during meetings with colleagues, staff, customers and the various interactions of every day life. An absolute must for anyone interested who needs to practise effective communication.

Carol Wilson, Creator with David Grove of www.cleancoaching.com

Towards the end of 2006 I decided to sample one of Wendy Sullivan and Judy Rees' courses in `Clean Language'. Little did I know that this `taster' would develop into a deep fascination, the start of a journey of learning that continues to unfold. Already I find I can use `Clean' in coaching and mentoring, in supporting student learning in Higher Education, and as a research tool.

Until now, there has been only one book about `Clean Language', James Lawley and Penny Tompkins' excellent `Metaphors in Mind'. It is impossible, though, for a single volume to meet the needs of everyone who would like to learn about this exciting field (think of how many introductions to NLP are on the market!) so it is great to see Wendy and Judy increase the published literature by 100% at a stroke.

What Wendy and Judy provide in this volume reflects all the best qualities of their courses; clarity, practicality, fun and integrity, all presented in a way that is accessible, logically structured and great value. Phew. And with all that, it's something that should sell like what? Hot cakes, if you ask me.'

Dr Paul Tosey, School of Management, University of Surrey

What a relief to be able to move on to something as well-written, as coherently organised, and as generally competent as *Clean Language* by Sullivan and Rees. I couldn't imagine a much more thorough-going contrast.

Some purists may wonder why I've reviewed books on Clean Language (see also Metaphors in Mind, Lawley and Tompkins). And the answer is, "For the same reason that I've reviewed books like Lakoff and Johnson's book Metaphors We Live By. That is, because whilst these books aren't directly about NLP, they contain a great deal of information which it is useful for NLPers to know in order to enhance their NLP skills."

In the case of *Clean Language* (the book), the usefulness is particularly evident in chapters 3 and 7 - The Magic of Metaphor and Modelling Cleanly, respectively. It is certainly true that the ideas in this book are, as you might expect, to some extent out of sync with those of NLP. On the subject of modelling, for example, there is a clear intention in both approaches to keep the modeller's ideas, values, opinions, etc. out of the way of the modellee's processing. But whereas in NLP this is achieved (as far as possible) by collecting information at a subconscious level with no conscious evaluation of the model until the modelling process is complete, in clean languaging (if that is the right term) the whole process is conducted at a conscious level, but the facilitator's thoughts are kept out of the developing model, as far as possible, by only feeding back to the modeller/modellee (they are the same person) their own words. Done correctly, the facilitator excludes from their feedback questions all interpretation or paraphrasing of the modeller's words, hence the term "clean" language.

A further, and very important, aspect of this comparison is the difference between the two intended outcomes.

In NLP, the modeller is usually building a model to facilitate a transfer of skills between the modellee and one or more other people. In clean languaging the primary purpose, again if I have understood the process correctly, is to guide the modellee in their construction of an entirely personal metaphor from which they will gain information which will help them to better understand their own personality, behaviour, world-view, or whatever.

Obviously where there are differences in approach these can be largely attributed to the differences in the underlying intentions.

Back to this particular book, I've been wondering if there is any way that the authors could have given it greater appeal to a diverse audience. And I don't really see how they could.

I found the writing clear without over-simplification; there are plenty of script fragments illustrating various points; and plenty of "Activities" so that readers can immediately practise and apply what they have been reading about.

There are also numerous cartoons, some of them little more than thumbnail sketches which reflect the words of a subheading and help (for the benefit of the more visually-inclined) to break up what might otherwise be an overwhelming flood of words. Others, such as the cartoon on page 148, clarify the meaning of the surrounding text in a way that will save some readers (including me) from having to read the text two or three time to be sure of getting the right message.

Finally, as far as this review is concerned, I was much impressed by the obvious expertise of the two authors. This came across, for me, in little comments which may read common sense, but which are only likely to have come from personal experience, such as this comment on page 88:

"And remember that when working Cleanly, it's not the facilitator's job to make change happen. Any change that occurs comes from within the client and happens at the client's own pace, so that it fits them perfectly."

That's just one of the many things I enjoyed about reading this book, and why I've rated it:

Highly Recommended: * * * * * *

Andy Bradbury, Honest Abe's NLP Emporium
www.bradburyac.mistral.co.uk

Clean Language

Revealing Metaphors and Opening Minds

by Wendy Sullivan and Judy Rees

Crown House Publishing Limited
www.crownhouse.co.uk
www.crownhousepublishing.com

First published by
Crown House Publishing Ltd
Crown Buildings, Bancyfelin, Carmarthen, Wales, SA33 5ND, UK
www.crownhouse.co.uk

and

Crown House Publishing Company LLC
6 Trowbridge Drive, Suite 5, Bethel, CT 06801, USA
www.crownhousepublishing.com

First published 2008. Reprinted 2009 (twice), 2010 and 2011.
Transferred to digital printing 2015.

Enquiries should be addressed to Crown House Publishing Limited.
British Library of Cataloguing-in-Publication Data
A catalogue entry for this book is available
from the British Library.

Print ISBN 978-184590125-7
Mobi ISBN 978-184590317-6
ePub ISBN 978-184590318-3

LCCN 2009931999

This book is dedicated to the memory of
David Grove, creator of Clean Language—
a creative genius and extraordinary healer

1 December 1950—8 January 2008

Contents

Acknowledgements

We have dedicated this book to David Grove, creator of Clean Language, in gratitude for his generosity in sharing this work with us and with the world. He offered his full support in the book's creation and we are sorry he did not live to see it published.

We are also massively indebted to Penny Tompkins and James Lawley. They made the writing of this book possible by their many years of work in this field, by their book *Metaphors in Mind*, and by the training, facilitation and ongoing support we have both received from them. They have spent a huge amount of time and energy studying the text and providing detailed feedback on it. We are eternally grateful to them.

We are also grateful to the wider Clean community within which we work and live. Individuals such as Cei Davies Linn, Phil Swallow, Caitlin Walker and Marian Way have made a considerable contribution to the development of the field and to our understanding of it.

We would like to thank the following people who offered feedback on the text: Judy Barber, Gina Campbell, Scott Downs, Charles Faulkner, Maggi Gilson, Nigel Heath, Annemiek van Helsdingen, Barbara Houseman, Margaret Meyer, Violetta Nowak, Rob Sullivan, Hans-Peter Wellke and Sue White.

A big 'thank you' is also due to the individuals and organisations who have allowed us to use their stories as examples in the book. Some are named in the text, others are not—whether named or not, we are very grateful.

We also thank our friends and colleagues for their support during the process of completing the book, Crown House for publishing it, Les Evans for his illustrations and Tom Fitton for his beautiful cover design.

Finally, thank you for picking up our book. We invite you to enjoy it, and any effects it may have!

Foreword

Our understanding of people is changing. According to Steven Pinker, and many other cognitive scientists, *'The Stuff of Thought'* is fundamentally metaphoric. No longer do we believe metaphor is only the province of poetry and prose. No longer do we believe metaphor is a rare add-on to ordinary speech. No longer do we believe abstract concepts are the way people make sense of the world. Why? Because metaphor is deeply embedded in, and essential to, language and thought. Whether we realise it or not, daily speech is peppered with metaphors, often several per minute.

We can't think, reason or interact without metaphor. Consider the internet for a moment. How could we understand it without metaphors such as the *worldwide web*, with its *pages, links, home, forward* and *backward navigation, pop-ups* and *drop-down menus*? The more complex the world becomes, the more we need to ground our ideas in embodied metaphors.

Slowly, people working in psychology, education, health and especially business, are waking up to the importance of metaphor. As examples of the latter, Gareth Morgan's *Images of Organization* (1986) and *Imaginization* (1993) were landmark books. More recently, Anne Miller wrote *Metaphorically Selling* (2004). Note that these books focus on the consultant's, or salesperson's, metaphors. By contrast, Gerald and Lindsay Zaltman's *Marketing Metaphoria* (2008) explains how consumers' metaphors count just as much. James Geary's forthcoming *I Is An Other: The Secret Life of Metaphor* will go further and show how metaphor is at work in all aspects of our personal, professional and social lives.

The significance of metaphor is being studied by academics working in the field of Cognitive Linguistics. This subject has been expanding since the launch of George Lakoff and Mark Johnson's *Metaphors We Live By* in 1980. Coincidentally, at about that time a

New Zealand counselling psychologist was embarking on a quest to help heal the minds of individuals using their *personal* metaphors. David Grove noticed his clients commonly used metaphor to describe their painful emotions, traumatic memories and deepest sense of who they were. He discovered that, once these metaphors were examined, they rapidly became idiosyncratic— there were elements and meaning that only applied to the individual. Furthermore, Grove noticed that each individual's metaphors had a structure and an internal logic that remained coherent and consistent over time. Rather than people *having* metaphors, it's as if they *were* their metaphors. And when these changed, they did too.

Grove was faced with a conundrum. If language is inherently metaphorical, how could he work with others' metaphors without bringing his own into the conversation? His solution, Clean Language, was a brilliant innovation—a simple set of questions that make use of only the most basic elements of human perception: space, event, category, attribution and intention. The *combination* of Clean Language with client-generated metaphors will be one of his enduring contributions.

Grove's early ideas were published as *Resolving Traumatic Memories: Metaphors and Symbols in Psychotherapy* (1989). The book was based on recorded conversations edited by Basil Panzer. It was another 11 years before we published our formulation *Metaphors in Mind: Transformation through Symbolic Modelling* (2000). More than a quarter of a century has passed since Grove embarked on his creative journey and it is a surprise that Wendy Sullivan and Judy Rees' book is only the third about his pioneering work.

While the Clean approach will be instantly valuable to therapists and coaches, *Clean Language: Revealing Metaphors and Opening Minds* also shows how it can be taken into conversations between parent and child, teacher and pupil, manager and staff, doctor and patient, researcher and subject; into team meetings, organisational development and many other areas. Along the way, the reader is made aware of how their own assumptions and intentions influence the systems in which they live, work and play.

This book is part of a rising wave of interest in, application of and research into metaphor. We applaud Wendy and Judy's willingness and enthusiasm to make this work available to a wider range of people by the publication of such a practical book.

James Lawley and Penny Tompkins
July 2008

Introduction

We needed to find a snappy story to open the book.

"What kind of snappy?" we wondered.

- Snappy like a smiling cartoon crocodile?
- Snappy like a game of cards?
- Snappy like the snap of fingers, instantly attracting attention?

When you think of a snappy story, what kind of snappy is *your* snappy story? We'll tell you about ours at the end of the chapter.

What happens when you think about these snappy stories? Each kind of snappy is a different metaphor – a different comparison of one thing (snappy) to another (crocodile, cards etc).

We do this kind of comparing all the time. That is, we think in metaphor[1]. Metaphors are fundamental to how we make sense of the world, and how we organise our thoughts, and yet we're not usually aware of our metaphors.

This book explores an unusual way of thinking about thinking which will enable you to grasp the importance of metaphor in thinking, in language, and in communication.

You'll learn how to use Clean Language questions to help other people to explore their thinking and the metaphors which underpin it. And as you get to grips with the material in this book, your own metaphors will emerge, opening up new realisations about yourself and the way you think.

---

[1] 'Metaphor' in this book includes analogies, similes, parables, metonymies, parallels, literary metaphors etc.

Using Clean Language can:

- Help people to make changes they would like in their lives
- Provide both you and them with valuable information about the way they think and how they do things
- Improve communication, understanding and rapport.

Other specific benefits often reported by Clean Language users include:

- It helps people do their best thinking, setting the scene for greater creativity and for new information to emerge
- It encourages people to take responsibility for themselves
- It empowers people to decide the way forward for themselves
- It honours each individual's uniqueness, making it especially valuable when diversity is an issue
- It can maximise collaboration and innovation
- It avoids 'leading the witness' while getting to the truth
- It enables you to talk another person's language, so that they feel acknowledged and heard
- It is flexible and can be used alongside a number of other approaches to improve their effectivness.

If your job involves gathering information from other people and/or assisting them to change, in almost any context, using Clean Language questions will help get better results.

Clean Language has its roots in therapy, but is branching into a wide range of other fields. It has been used successfully by coaches, mentors, consultants, managers, health professionals, parents, teachers, journalists, salespeople and people in many other occupations: the list keeps on growing. It seems that it can be used in almost any field of human endeavour.

Clean Language is useful in one-to-one situations and with groups, in formal settings and in casual conversations. By using Clean Language, you and those you spend time with can expect to make better decisions based on more complete information, and so achieve goals more easily.

- "This amazingly powerful tool could transform the way we interact, and run meetings and appraisals, within our business."—Caroline Frost, Director of Marketing and Training, Informa Healthcare

- "We've used Clean Language as a co-coaching model for 250 senior managers and it's gone down a storm."—Lorenza Clifford, personal and team development consultant, Pricewater houseCoopers

- "It gives you the confidence to really get results with your clients."—Mark Hawkswell, coach and trainer

- "When you use Clean Language in the classroom be prepared for a leap in learning. Colleagues have been surprised by the speed of impact. Children learn to think deeply and to express their ideas with clarity. They come to appreciate each other's specialness and to value differences. They learn to think about thinking and become more comfortable exploring challenging ideas... especially their own!"—Julie McCracken, primary school teacher

- "Clean Language is a simple yet amazing set of tools that is effective in unlocking a client's assumptions, communication, and thinking. This powerful process is a must for anyone involved in the coaching, managing or teaching profession."—Steve Nobel, author, coach, and a director of Alternatives.

- "Clean Language is a fantastic tool. It's so versatile and so respectful."—Sheena Bailey, management consultant to UK health services

- "Clean Language should be on the curriculum of every secondary school in Great Britain. It will boost confidence and give anyone a much greater understanding of what it really means to be human."—Pamela Hadfield, learning consultant working with teenagers

- "Quite often, projects succeed in building to the requirements on paper, but still fail to meet the client's expectations. It's early days, but I think using Clean Language is leading to better results, and more aligned expectations of what is going to be built." Roland Hill, IT business analyst, IPROFS, Netherlands.

Clean Language is simple, and yet has fascinating implications.

At the most simple level, Clean Language is a set of twelve questions from which assumptions and metaphors have been 'cleansed' as far as possible. These questions are good for obtaining information from another person in a structured way that helps you and them to get a really clear understanding of what they mean.

As a complete approach, Clean Language can be combined with the metaphors a person uses, creating a bridge between their conscious and unconscious minds. This can become a profound personal exploration: a route to deeper understanding of themselves, to transcending limiting beliefs and behaviours, and to resolution and healing. The person asking Clean Language questions gets a new understanding of people, and even of the nature of consciousness.

It often surprises beginners to find that the same twelve questions and the same basic principles are used at both the simple level and when using the complete approach. This makes Clean Language very flexible.

Clean Language isn't useful all the time. Clean is not a persuasion tool, although it can certainly help you to understand what will convince someone. It's not a good way to force people to change against their will. It is not a method of interpreting metaphors. It may not be the best approach in an emergency or at times when you are delivering specific information. And it can be extremely useful in a wide range of other contexts.

This book is an introduction, to equip you to take your first steps on a journey. We hope it will whet your appetite for more learning, and we've included details of further resources later in the book.[2]

Some people find that Clean Language comes naturally to them, and that they can relax into asking the Clean Language questions in lots of different situations, right from the start. Others find it takes a little longer. The fact you've picked up this book means you're interested, which is really all that's needed.

---

[2] For readers with an appetite for theory, a short essay, '*Theoretical Underpinnings of Symbolic Modelling*' by Judy Rees, is available online at http://www.cleanchange.co.uk

Whether you want to become a more involved parent, a better salesperson, a great coach, to extend your creative or spiritual awareness, or just to understand yourself and others more fully, learning Clean Language will be valuable.

About us

The two of us—Wendy Sullivan and Judy Rees—are passionate about Clean Language and its effects. We've both been convinced by our personal, real-life experience.

Judy was a news journalist and media executive who worked in newspapers, TV and new media. She fell in love with Clean Language in 2003: as a writer and reporter, she found the way it used metaphor particularly fascinating. A lifelong workaholic with few outside interests, she experienced a major personal crisis when her employers downsized and she faced redundancy—combined with the loss of her partner, her home and most of her friends. Clean Language coaching helped her to find a way out of that fear-filled place and to discover a route to a more balanced lifestyle, including close relationships, wide interests, and a new career. She now works alongside Wendy as a Clean Language facilitator and trainer, and develops new applications for Clean Language in business and other contexts.

Wendy has been working with Clean Language since 1997. Encountering it for the first time in a conference presentation, she discovered an inspiring personal metaphor—a lighthouse. When she excitedly told her husband about it later, he made a teasing comment, "Oh – so you can only focus on a tiny part of your life at any one time – and that only momentarily!" Wendy was surprised to discover how strongly she felt that this was not something to joke about – that the lighthouse represented something key about who she was and how she did things: how she was able to concentrate her own attention, and how she helped others to direct theirs in useful ways. She realised that it had taken only a small number of Clean Language questions to reveal core information that had remained hidden in spite of all her personal development over the years. It was clear to her that she wanted to master Clean Language skills and start using it in her work with people as quickly as possible.

Wendy's background is in speech and language therapy, but she is now a specialist in training people to use Clean Language on open courses and within companies. She also uses Clean in working as a coach, trainer, facilitator and psychotherapist. Her former students on five continents are now using Clean Language in their work.

About Clean Language and its developers

The Clean Language questions were developed by an inspiring counseling psychologist, David Grove, as he worked with trauma victims during the 1980s and 1990s. In contrast to the fashion of the time, he resisted the temptation to give advice, honoured his clients' choice of words rather than paraphrasing, and devised questions which contained as few assumptions and metaphors as possible. This approach helped people to work with their own metaphors, enabling them to explore their experience indirectly in ways that allowed them to heal and move on.

David, who was part-Maori, came from New Zealand and spent much of his life on the move. He trained many thousands of therapists in his 'Grovian Metaphor Therapy' at workshops worldwide, particularly in the UK, USA, Australia, New Zealand and Ireland. He was visiting faculty at Durham, Manchester and Edinburgh Universities and a score of US Universities included his work in their courses. He co-authored a book, *Resolving Traumatic Memories*[3], with B.I. Panzer, created a number of video and tape sets, and for most of the 1990s ran a retreat centre in Eldon, Missouri.

---

[3] Obviously learning Clean Language from a book does not make you a therapist. Use what you learn here only in ways which are appropriate for your qualifications and experience. If you are in any doubt about your competence to deal with an issue, refer to an appropriate professional.

James Lawley and Penny Tompkins were inspired by the effectiveness of David's healing work. They codified his approach and extended it, making it more accessible to a wider range of users. They called their work Symbolic Modelling, and their comprehensive book on the subject, *Metaphors in Mind: Transformation Through Symbolic Modelling*, was published in 2000.

Now we, along with others, are working to make Clean Language still more accessible to people worldwide.

David Grove's original work, and Penny and James's subsequent developments, take a revolutionary view of the way people think and communicate, and provide a set of tools which has the potential to change many lives for the better, way beyond their origin in clinical therapy.

In this book we'll use the word 'Clean' both as an abbreviated label for David, Penny and James's work and its derivatives, and to indicate the philosophical approach which underpins them. We'll explain more about this later.

About this book

This book is an introduction to Clean Language. It will be a practical workbook for beginners, as well as a reference guide for Clean Language facilitators who have some experience. We begin with simple ideas and simple activities that require no prior knowledge, moving on to more complex ones.

Chapter 1 offers a brief overview of the principles of Clean Language. The three chapters which follow look in detail at three of the principles—asking Clean Language questions, working with personal metaphors, and listening exquisitely.

In Chapters 5 and 6 we go through the 12 basic Clean Language questions in detail, explaining how they are used.

Chapter 7 looks at the use of Clean Language in modelling for finding out how someone does something, while Chapters 8 and 9 consider its use in contexts where change is wanted. Modelling and change are the principal applications of Clean Language.

At this point, you will be all set to use what you have learnt to facilitate yourself, so we provide activities for this in Chapter 10.

From here, with the basics in place, Chapters 11-13 will help you to fine-tune your skills as you start to use them to help others make the changes they would like. You will learn how to direct attention more precisely and how to make use of space.

Finally, to inspire you to use Clean Language in your own life, in Chapters 14 and 15 we give some more detailed descriptions of contexts where it has already been used.

To help you, we have used different kinds of bullet points to mark out different kinds of information.

❖ Denotes an example of Clean Language being used in real life
− Denotes a Clean Language question

Throughout, we will suggest activities for you to do. They are integral to learning Clean Language and by doing them you'll get information which is not provided elsewhere, including a sense of how it feels to ask, and to be asked, the Clean Language questions. So please do them! If you read the book but don't have the experiences you may draw inaccurate conclusions about how engaging the process is.

Some of the activities can be done alone, while others need a partner. Sharing the activities with others will bring the maximum benefit.

We've also included transcripts to illustrate specific sections. While some have been edited slightly to help you grasp the point being made, they are the best way to see how Clean Language has been used in real situations.

Our snappy story

Remember the search for a snappy story to open the book? We (Wendy and Judy) used Clean Language to help us to find the kind of snappy story that was right for us.

We started by exploring what we each wanted to happen. Judy wanted the knowledge the book contains to be like a ball of golden light which could be passed from person to person—leaving each person's hands full of light as it left them. Wendy imagined a globe with a network of bright connections: as each new connection was made, it exploded in dozens of new directions. Like the lighting of a sparkler, each new spark potentially became the hub of a new explosion, a new network.

As the conversation continued, we turned our attention to what we wanted the effects of the book to be. As we discussed our hopes and plans it became clear to us that we wanted its launch to be like the arrival of the digital camera. Remember the switch from film cameras to digital photography? In the days of film, there were some excellent photographers—but most people took relatively few pictures, and those we took were often quite uninspiring.

Once we'd got the hang of our digital cameras, though, all that changed. Nowadays, everyone has the freedom to take lots and lots of pictures—and the more we practice, the better the pictures become. Becoming a good photographer is within everyone's reach. We can also snap away in 'difficult' conditions, such as low light—and if it doesn't produce a top-class picture every time there's no harm done. We even have cameras in our telephones that are small enough to carry everywhere and use at any time, without preparation.

We'd like this book and its effects to be like that. It is designed to put Clean Language in people's hands, worldwide, ready to be used whenever it could be valuable. Enjoy!

Chapter 1
Getting Started

"No-one ever listened themselves out of a job"
—*Calvin Coolidge, US president*

Clean Language amounts to a new way of thinking about the way people think, with profound implications and powerful effects. And the basics are simple.

Typically two people are involved. The questioner asks Clean Language questions and the speaker answers.

There are twelve basic Clean Language questions, which are combined with words used by the speaker. That makes the questions as flexible as the notes of the musical scale, which can be used to create anything from a nursery rhyme to a pop song or an orchestral symphony.

As Clean Language questioner:

- Listen attentively
- Remember that your assumptions, opinions and advice are your own
- Ask Clean Language questions to explore a person's words, particularly their metaphors
- Listen to the answers and then ask more Clean Language questions about what they have said.

If a person is seeking to change, then change happens naturally as part of the process. This isn't a method for forcing anyone to change.

The same approach, with the same questions, can be used wherever you're gathering information—anything from a recruitment interview to a corporate best-practice project, to finding out what your child did at school today.

The Clean Language process

To introduce the principles of Clean Language, we are going to begin with the two most commonly used, and most versatile, Clean Language questions:

– *(And) what kind of X (is that X)?*
– *(And) is there anything else about X?*

The 'X' in the question refers to a word or phrase the speaker has used.

For example, in the introduction we wrote about a snappy story and asked:

– What kind of snappy?

We could also have asked:

– And is there anything else about that snappy?

 Using a person's own words in your question shows that you have really been listening. Don't paraphrase—parrot-phrase! People's words are important to them, and using their words tends to help them feel respected and acknowledged. You'll be surprised how easy this soon becomes.

Both questions encourage the person to elaborate on their experience, to find out more about it. The question 'What kind of X?' invites them to 'zoom in' on the specific details, while 'Anything else about X?' can help them 'zoom out' to the wider context or to focus on other details about 'X'. Both these questions can be usefully asked about more or less anything, any time. So keep them handy!

❖ A mother who had just learned some Clean Language picked up her daughter Jenny from school. When Jenny showed her a picture of a house she had drawn, Mum asked, "What kind of house is that house?", "And is there anything else about that house?" and so on. What resulted was one of the longest after-school conversations they'd ever enjoyed. The next day after school, Jenny demanded: "Ask me some more questions, Mummy!"

❖ It seemed as if the meeting had been going on for ages, but at last the discussion seemed to be moving forward. Then the sales director said, "I think we're at breaking point." Margaret, who was in the chair, felt herself becoming annoyed, why on earth did the director think the meeting was on the point of break-down? She remembered her Clean Language and asked, "What kind of breaking point is that?" "The point of breaking through," the director said. Margaret was relieved to have been wrong! The meeting moved quickly forward to a resolution.

What's special about Clean Language questions?

The two Clean Language questions we have just introduced sound very ordinary. So what's special about them? One way to understand this is to compare them with two commonly-used questioning categories—Open and Closed questions.

Type of question	Closed question	Open question	Clean Language question
Example	Do you like X?	What are you going to do about X?	What kind of X (is that X)?
Response	Yes or No	Responds with one or more actions	Responds with specific information in whichever way they prefer

Closed questions limit the speaker to a yes/no answer and tend to close down the topic. Open questions invite more than a yes/no answer, adding detail to the topic. So the effect of Clean Language questions is similar to that of open questions.

3

What's special about Clean Language questions is that they have been pared down to contain as few assumptions and metaphors as possible. This makes them 'ultra-Open', allowing the speaker the maximum freedom to choose how they will answer.

Go for the good stuff

Asking Clean Language questions about a person's experience tends to bring it to life for them, so that it feels very real. This is particularly true when asking about a person's metaphors. And because of this, it's important to 'go for the good stuff'.

We strongly recommend that you ask the questions predominantly about the *positive* aspects of a person's experience. The best aspects of themselves, their hopes for the future and their metaphors for these are the kind of things they would want to be 'brought to life'. Do this and you're likely to find things moving forward, fast.

As a beginner, it's best to avoid using Clean Language to explore problems or unhappy experiences, since asking the questions can bring these to life, too. This can lead to the speaker becoming stuck in their problem and feeling that they have few options, and so is likely to be less effective at helping them to change things.

Whenever you use Clean Language, it's worth being aware of your intention from the outset. Are you:

- Gathering information for your own benefit?
- Gathering information for someone else's benefit (e.g. as a researcher)?
- Helping another person to become clear about something or to understand themselves?
- Helping another person to make a change in their life?

The Clean Language process is fundamentally the same in all these cases, although there can be subtle differences in how the questions are used.

Being aware of your intention will help you to ensure you use Clean Language only when it is ethical to do so. Clean Language is not intended as a tool for manipulating others.

Metaphors are everywhere

Clean Language questions *can* be asked about anything a person says, but they were designed for exploring the metaphors which underpin people's thinking.

Metaphor is fundamental to the process of thinking. Whenever we compare one thing to another, whether we are aware of doing so or not, we are thinking in metaphor. And whenever we describe one thing in terms of another, we are speaking in metaphor. Metaphoric thought and metaphoric language go hand in hand.

Here are a few examples of metaphors. Some ways of talking about relationships[4] are:

- Look *how far* we've come.
- We're *at a crossroads*.
- We'll just have to *go our separate ways*.
- We can't *turn back* now.
- I don't think this relationship is *going anywhere*.
- *Where are* we?
- We're *stuck*.
- It's been a *long, bumpy road*.
- Our marriage is *on the rocks*.
- This relationship is *foundering*.

These statements must be metaphorical: a relationship cannot literally be on rocks, nor stand at a crossroads. In all these examples the relationship is being described in terms of a journey. A journey is one of the common metaphors used for relationships (and for many other things)—and it is by no means the only one.

---

[4] Taken from George Lakoff and Mark Johnson, *Metaphors We Live By*, 1980.

Some other examples of metaphors for relationships include:

- Our relationship is all-consuming
- It's a marriage made in heaven
- This is a close partnership
- We support each other.

Becoming aware of metaphors is the first step towards exploring them, and to helping others to explore their own. We'll discuss metaphors in greater depth later.

Activity: Practising the first two questions

Visit a shop that sells something you might be interested in buying. See how much information you can gather by asking the assistant:

- *What kind of X (is that X)?*
- *Is there anything else about X?*

where 'X' is the purchase item, a part of it or something about one of its functions.

* * *

What did you discover about how many times you could ask those questions?

Now that you have had a taste of the riches that Clean Language offers, it is time to explore the principles of Clean Language. We begin by focusing further on asking questions—especially Clean Language questions—and why it is a worthwhile approach.

Chapter 2
Great Questions!

"It is not the answer that enlightens, but the question"
—Eugene Ionesco

It's natural that we want to help others. Whenever we find people in trouble or distress, what could be kinder than to reach out and try to fix the problem? This impulse has been described as the 'righting reflex'—a reflex that causes us to want to 'put things right'. This urge to solve other people's problems can be one of our biggest preoccupations. The question "How can I help here?" is constantly in many people's minds.

Of course, there can be great value in charitable giving, or a helping hand with the heavy lifting. Often, though, we try to help by offering advice based on our own experience. And advice may not be helpful.

Have you ever thought you've given excellent advice that the other person didn't follow? How often have you followed advice which you didn't ask for? We've asked this of a number of groups and their answers have varied all the way from 'rarely' to 'never'.

Activity: "If I were you ..."

For this exercise you'll need a partner and two difficulties each (we suggest you choose minor ones). For example: "I'm playing too many computer games" or "I haven't done my ironing".

Ask your partner to state their difficulty. Now you respond with one minute's worth of your very best advice, "If I were you, I'd...", "What you need to do is ...", "Have you tried ...", etc.

Then ask your partner to state their second difficulty. This time, you respond by repeating back some or all of their words and asking some or all of these Clean Language questions:

— *What would you like to have happen?*

and/or

— *What needs to happen?*

and/or

— *Is there anything else that needs to happen?*

For example, "Oh, you haven't done your ironing and you want to get it done. What needs to happen for you to get it done?"

Swap roles and repeat.

What did you notice as the questioner:

- Was it hard to think of suitable advice?
- Was it difficult not to give advice in the second conversation?
- Did you find that the responsibility for solving the problem shifted?

As the speaker:

- Which conversation has the most potential for resolving your difficulty?
- Did you find yourself arguing with the advice?
- Which conversation made you think more deeply (and perhaps more honestly) about your difficulty and how to resolve it?

The three common reasons that advice is not followed are:

1. The advisor is providing a solution to the wrong problem. For example, one person's suggested solution when faced with being overweight would relate to solving the problem of how to get to the gym more regularly, while another might want to solve the problem of how to eat less.

2. The advisor is highlighting the wrong benefits of solving the problem. For one person, reaching their ideal weight is all about looking fantastic and attracting the perfect partner, while for another it might be about being able to enjoy high-adrenaline

sports. Telling the adrenaline junkie that counting their calories will make them look fantastic may not motivate them at all.

3. The 'advisee' is of two minds: one part wants to do something while another doesn't. For example, part might want to reach their ideal weight, but another part prefers to eat cream cakes and doughnuts. If someone advises using a calorie counter, which part will make the most noise? It will be the 'cakes and doughnuts' part, which can probably offer a number of good reasons *not* to count calories—to the extent that it might talk the person right out of doing anything useful about their weight— which is the exact reverse of what the advisor intended.

Clean recognises that advice isn't always—or even often— an answer to the stated problem. So instead of advising, Clean Language users ask great questions!

❖ When Wendy was running 'Train the Trainer' courses, participants sometimes said they were nervous about delivering training. It would have been easy for her to assume they wanted to feel confident, and for her to give advice on how to look/be more confident, "Stand solidly on both feet to be well-grounded, make eye contact with your participants," and so on.

But when the participants were asked the Clean Language question, "And what would you like to have happen?" they said,

- "I need techniques for dealing with difficult participants."
- "I'd be fine if I could work out how to get the content clear in my mind."
- "I want my face to stay normal (not blush)."
- "I want to enjoy training."

So while Wendy's confidence-building advice might have been good in general, it wouldn't necessarily have helped these people to achieve their desired outcomes.

Each person knows more about their own challenges than anyone else. Their problem-solving ideas will fit themselves and their problems perfectly—someone else's may not. And their *own* ideas are more likely to motivate and empower them to take action. Their ideas will continue to work when the advisor is not there to give advice because Clean Language questions encourage people to think for themselves.

So, whenever you use Clean Language, keep your advice to yourself. This idea isn't new. Active listening, rather than advising, forms the basis of most modern coaching and management practice. Top salespeople have a saying, "When you're telling, you're not selling." In Clean Language, listening is so central that we've included an entire chapter on it later in the book.

Even the best listeners can unwittingly put ideas and suggestions into the minds of others—it can be so subtle that people don't know they are doing it. Clean Language provides a structure within which people can *really* keep their advice (and opinions) to themselves. They use *only* the other person's words and the Clean Language questions to get results.

The Clean Language questions have been honed and polished over the years to reduce the number of assumptions and metaphors they contain. This minimises the amount of 'contamination' from the questioner, freeing up the resources of the person being questioned so that they can think effectively for themselves.

Behaving Cleanly

The practice of keeping your advice, opinions and assumptions to yourself, and listening and observing with your full attention on the other person's words (and non-verbal signals), is known as 'behaving Cleanly'. It's central to Clean Language.

In reality, it's impossible to be 'perfectly' Clean. You can't *not* affect someone's attention whenever you speak to them, since all communication directs attention in some way. A simple greeting such as "Good morning!" is often intended to change how the other person is feeling, however slightly.

Of course, there are many situations where it is appropriate not to use Clean Language, situations in which you have every right—and possibly a duty—to voice your opinions. For example, "That hurts!" is something that needs to be said.

It's even possible to use Clean Language questions in a not-Clean way, that is, with an intention to manipulate. For example, later in the book you'll discover how to use Clean Language and metaphor to help someone find out more about a positive state—happiness, for example, which usually leads to them experiencing it there and then, feeling happier. But did you get the person's permission to cheer them up in this way? Was that what they wanted? In what circumstances would cheering them up be absolutely reasonable, and when might it be manipulative?

When you use Clean Language, it is important to consider:

- What does the other person want?
- What is my intention in this situation? To 'stay Clean' or to influence?
- Do I have their permission (implied or explicit) to obtain information from them or to help them to change?
- Am I able to work constructively in this situation? If not, what needs to happen?

Clean Language comes from the world of psychotherapy, but by itself it won't make you a psychotherapist. If you are in any doubt about your competence to deal with an issue which arises, refer the person to an appropriate professional.

One of the things you'll gain from this book is the flexibility to choose to behave Cleanly and to notice when you are behaving in another way.

There's more to being an excellent Clean facilitator than this principle, but it's a great start. So, if you haven't already, begin practising behaving Clean straight away.

Times to use Clean Language:	**Times to use other language:**
• When the person you're working with is deeply engrossed in their inner world.	• When there is an emergency and you decide to take charge.
• When you want them to take responsibility for their own choices.	• When you hold a specific piece of information the other person needs and seems to be missing.
• When you want them to do their best thinking.	• When asked directly for your opinion.
• When you haven't yet had the opportunity to build up a really good understanding of what is going on for them.	• When your personal beliefs and values make it hard for you to keep your opinion to yourself.

Clean Language questions: Getting a name and address

You've already been introduced to two of the most useful Clean Language questions:

- *(And) what kind of X (is that X)?*
- *(And) is there anything else about X?*

With these and the question:

- *(And) where is X?* or *(And) whereabouts is X?*

you are equipped to get a 'name and address' using Clean Language questions.

Just as we get someone's name and address in order to stay in touch with them, in this process the questioner wants to get equivalent information about the things the speaker mentions, so that they can be referred to later.

The three questions:

- *(And) what kind of X (is that X)?*
- *(And) is there anything else about X?*
- *(And) where is X? or (And) whereabouts is X?*

can be asked about almost anything, any time, so keep them handy. Remember, 'X' represents one or more of the words the other person has used.

Once you know *what* something is (its name) and *where* it is (its address) then you can:

- remember it easily
- make a quick, precise note of it
- stay in touch with it
- reveal connections between it and other things
- refer to it and expect the other person to know what you are talking about
- return to it easily if you need to do so in future.

The word 'and' in all the Clean Language questions, and the phrase 'is that X' in the question "(And) what kind of X (is that X)?" are optional. Include them or not, depending on the context. Later, we'll explain more about how their use or omission can be used to direct attention.

❖ For example, in a gadget shop, the salesperson might say, "It's the new model. It has an extra-clear display." You could ask, "Is there anything else about the display?", "What kind of display?" and/or, "Whereabouts is the display?"

The Name and Address Questions encourage a person to elaborate about the thing they've mentioned to give more details. These questions are so important in Clean Language that we are offering several activities to help you practise the Name and Address Questions.

Activity: Think of a flower

Think of a flower.
What kind of flower is your flower? Take a moment to make a few notes. Now ask someone else to think of a flower, and then ask:

"What kind of flower is that flower?"
"Is there anything else about that flower?" and/or
"Where is that flower?"

Then try someone else. No two flowers will be identical. All the flowers will be different from the one you are thinking of. They could be any of hundreds of species. They could be any colour or size. In your mind's eye your flower could be in a particular location in relation to you, or imagined on its own or in a particular context. It could look 'real' or be like a photograph or a cartoon. Very soon the number of potential differences outweighs the similarities between different people's flowers.

And yet, when someone mentions 'a flower', we think we know what they mean.

Now do the activity again but this time start by thinking of a meeting. What kind of meeting is your meeting? Now ask someone else. How many kinds of meeting can you find?

Activity: Getting names and addresses

You will need a partner for this. To start with, each of you should think about a hobby or pastime you enjoy.

First ask your partner the ordinary question, "What hobby or pastime do you enjoy?"

You then have a couple of minutes to find out more about the hobby, using only the Clean Language questions:

– *(And) is there anything else about X?*
– *(And) what kind of X (is that X)?*
– *(And) where is X? or (And) whereabouts is X?*

combined with the person's own words.

The questions can be asked several times, in any order, about any aspect of what your partner has said.

After two or three minutes, swap roles.

Example transcript: Strong but flexible confident

Speaker:	I want to feel confident.
Questioner:	And what kind of confident?
Speaker:	Strong, but flexible. *(Name)*
Questioner:	And is there anything else about the 'strong but flexible' of that 'confident'?
Speaker:	It is what I want more of all the time.
Questioner:	And when you feel strong but flexible confident, where do you feel it?
Speaker:	In my chest. *(Address)*
Questioner:	Whereabouts in your chest?
Speaker:	In the centre. *(Address)*
Questioner:	And is there anything else about the strong but flexible confident in the centre of your chest?
Speaker:	I'm beginning to feel it right now …

In this transcript, the questioner establishes a name ("strong but flexible") and an address ("in the centre of my chest") for "confident". Notice how asking 'where' and then 'whereabouts' results in the speaker accessing more specific information about the location of "confidence".

Filling in the gaps

We are 'meaning-making' beings. We fill in the gaps in our knowledge of what, precisely, others mean. One way we do this is to imagine that their 'flower' is the same as ours. We frequently don't even think to check this. In most situations when two people have a conversation this 'filling in the gaps' is very handy. If we needed to check what everyone meant by 'flower' each time anyone mentioned one, a quick chat would be hard work. However, this shortcut can easily lead us down the wrong path.

What kind of 'filling in' is your 'filling in the gaps'?

Making assumptions is sensible and necessary in everyday life. It's useful to assume that our keys are where we left them and that when a waiter says, "Can I take your order?" it's appropriate to ask for food, not curtains or a car. But the fact is we can't be sure—we're filling in the gaps in our knowledge with information we have made up.

Most of us have long stopped noticing that we're doing any 'filling in' at all. We come to believe that the way we see the world is the way it 'really' is. With this attitude, we rarely think to ask for clarification, or to question any puzzling communication, and this can lead to the possibility of big, unnecessary misunderstandings.

All the Clean Language questions help to reduce misunderstandings. And the most useful ones for that are the Name and Address Questions, which clarify *what* the person is thinking about and *where* it is. And as you now know about Name and Address Questions, we are now going to focus on how to ask them.

Asking Name and Address Questions

The Name and Address Questions are:

– *(And) what kind of X (is that X)?*
– *(And) is there anything else about X?*
– *(And) where is X?* or *(And) whereabouts is X?*

Asking them is straightforward. Notice something your conversational partner has mentioned and ask one or both of these questions:

– *(And) what kind of X (is that X)?*
– *(And) is there anything else about X?*

replacing 'X' with their word or words.

You can ask the questions in any order, as many times as you like. After a question or two they will probably become quite specific about what they're saying: for example, "a tall, yellow sunflower". Now they have given it a 'name'.

Then you might ask:

– *(And) where is X?* or
– *(And) whereabouts is X?*

If there's a 'something' in someone's thoughts, it is fairly certain to be located 'somewhere', since space is a universally-used metaphor. There are several purposes for asking the 'location' questions. They help the person know where their 'somethings', or symbols are, and may lead to them becoming aware of additional information. Asking for an address will also help you as the questionner to know where symbols are, which will make it easy for you to refer to them.

You can choose whether to use the word 'where' or 'whereabouts' in your question, depending on the context, and what seems more natural for you and the person you're working with. Although it isn't universally so, it is common for people to interpret 'whereabouts?' to be asking for more specific information than 'where?'

Location questions are very valuable and questioners seldom ask too many of them. In fact, it is often useful to ask more than one location question in succession to help the speaker, and you, to become increasingly specific about where something is.

The Name and Address Questions can be used about all kinds of things, whether they are real or imaginary. Imaginary things do have locations. For example, your keys might be located on the real table beside you, where you and others can see them and touch them, and the flower that you thought of earlier might be in an imaginary field in your mind's eye, and you might imagine it as being to one side of you, perhaps in much the same space as the table with the keys.

As a rule, asking:

- *"What kind of?"* will elicit the name of a symbol—the information which distinguishes it from any other symbol.

- *"Where?"* or *"Whereabouts?"* will get the location of the symbol.

- *"Anything else?"* can be asked about anything, anywhere.

- ❖ Fran was organising a party and wanted to make sure the arrangements were exactly as she imagined them. Her friend Mary asked her the Name and Address Questions (e.g. "What kind of nibbles?" "Is there anything else about nibbles?" and "Whereabouts are nibbles?") to help her create a very detailed specification for the caterers.

- ❖ An executive was trying to sort out a complex situation with the help of his coach. "It's all muddled up in my head," he said. She asked, "Whereabouts in your head?", "Well, I suppose if it's any- where, it's in the back of my head." "And whereabouts in the back of your head?", "Well, on the left, about *here.*" As the ses- sion continued, the executive discovered that different aspects of the situation were in slightly different places—the first step in sorting out the muddle and getting clear about his next steps.

Now that you have a flavour of some of the Clean Language questions, we are going to turn our attention in the next chapter to metaphor and its role in the Clean process. To get a taste of Clean Language questions used with metaphor, we suggest the activity below.

Activity: Listening like what?

Use Clean Language questions to develop a metaphor of what it is like when you are listening at your best. Here's how:

1. Ask yourself, "When I am listening at my best, that's like what?"

For example, it might be like:

- A bright spotlight illuminating the person who is speaking
- A heart-to-heart connection
- The speaker's voice rings out loud and clear and other sounds are muffled.

Probably your metaphor is quite different from these examples. Whatever it is like for you is fine. There's no wrong personal metaphor. Whatever your metaphor is, value it.

2. Then ask yourself the Name and Address Questions:
– *(And) what kind of X (is that X)?*
– *(And) is there anything else about X?*

and

– *(And) where is X? or (And) whereabouts is X?*

a few times, in any order, where 'X' is your metaphor or a part of it.

Using the example metaphors above, questions could be:

"And when it is like a bright spotlight, what kind of spotlight is that bright spotlight?"

"And when it's like heart-to-heart connection, is there anything else about that connection?"

"And when it rings out loud and clear, whereabouts is that clear?"

If you are working with a friend, swap roles after a number of Name and Address Questions have been asked.

3. As you discover more about your metaphor for listening, start to notice any opportunities in everyday life for you to listen in this way. You may be surprised by the benefits of listening in this way.

In the days and weeks after completing this exercise, notice whether you have any of these commonly-reported experiences:

- Does your metaphor come to mind when you are in a situation that calls for good listening?
- Have you found yourself becoming aware of additional information relating to your metaphor, even when you have not been actively aiming to explore it further?

Chapter 3
The Magic of Metaphor

"Metaphor, that's how the whole fabric of mental interconnections holds together. Metaphor is right at the bottom of being alive"
—Gregory Bateson

Metaphor is at the heart of the Clean way of thinking. It is the main thing that sets it apart from other approaches based on facilitative questioning and listening.

Paying attention to metaphor will supercharge the results you get from your communication using Clean Language because:

- Metaphors condense information, making things more tangible and easier to work with.
- Metaphors can represent experience more fully than abstract concepts, and enable more effective communication.
- Metaphors allow us to think in deeper and more profound ways.
- Someone's metaphor for an experience has a similar structure to the experience that it represents.
- When people experience change, both their metaphor and their life experience generally associated with it change in tandem.

"The essence of metaphor is understanding and experiencing one kind of thing in terms of another," write Lakoff and Johnson.[5] Whenever one thing is described in terms of another, that's a metaphor. This definition of metaphor includes similes, parables, analogies, parallels metonymy, literary metaphors, etc.

The word 'metaphor' comes from the Greek 'amphora', a storage container used for transporting valuable goods. Since we use

---

[5] George Lakoff and Mark Johnson, *Metaphors We Live By,* 1980.

21

metaphor as a way to transport meaning from one kind of thing to another, the word 'metaphor' is itself a metaphor.

As human beings, we seem to be hardwired to think in metaphor, and to communicate using metaphor. And, as generations of story-tellers, leaders and salespeople have discovered, we are also hardwired to respond to metaphor—often unconsciously.

Activity: Coins

Take a handful of coins from your pocket, and look at them.

Notice their different shapes, colours and weights. Notice the jangling sound they make. What do they mean to you?

Now take those same coins and arrange them to represent you and your family or closest friends.

Imagine that (for reasons beyond your control) one of them has to be removed. Which one do you choose to remove?

What just happened? Take a moment to reflect on your experience before reading on.

* * *

Put that coin back where it belongs, if you removed it.

You probably had no difficulty representing people using coins. In other words, you knew how to use the coins as a metaphor for people. You didn't need much explanation because metaphor is 'hardwired' into your system.

For most people, once the coins had taken on that metaphoric representation, taking one away had emotional significance, at least to some degree. It seems that by thinking and speaking in metaphor, people trigger a more embodied, emotionally-rich experience than when using abstract language. Metaphor gets to the heart of things.

Now take a moment to notice what principles you used to do this activity. How did you choose what coin represented which person? Was the size of the coins significant? The colour? And what about the spatial arrangement? These are all different ways to symbolically represent relationships between people. If you ask a friend to do this activity, they will use some different attributes of the coins. But it is a safe bet that both you and they used location, with relative distance between coins indicating the 'closeness' of the relationship or the physical proximity of the people. As we said earlier, space is the most universal metaphor.

This activity was devised by Penny Tompkins and James Lawley

Because we think in metaphor, we speak and write in metaphor. Everyday language is bursting with metaphor—it has been suggested that people use roughly six metaphors a minute in normal conversation[6]. Our experience suggests we might use even more than this: almost all language is metaphorical at some level.

Especially when we need to describe abstract, complex or emotional things we are likely to reach for the familiarity of a more concrete metaphor.

Metaphors in language

Information transmitted in language can be regarded as fitting into three categories: sensory, abstract or metaphoric.

---

[6] Raymond W. Gibbs Jr., 'Categorization and metaphor understanding'. *Psychological Review* 99, (3): 572-577, 1992.

Distinguishing between sensory, conceptual and metaphoric information will help you to spot the metaphors that people use, and asking Clean Language questions of their metaphor will in turn improve your skill with Clean Language.

Sensory information relates to the five senses: seeing, hearing, feeling/touching, tasting and smelling. The colour, sound, texture and smell of the coins are all pieces of sensory information.

Abstract information consists of concepts, thoughts and 'labels' which are not based in the senses and include categorisations and expressions of beliefs and emotions.

Some responses to a handful of coins might be:

- They are worth everything and nothing
- I can buy a cup of tea with them
- I don't know what to do with them
- They are interesting
- They are more valuable than I realised
- I hate having such a lot of change.

Metaphoric expressions describe one kind of thing in terms of another. Very often the metaphors say more about a person's thinking than all their conceptual words put together.

- We're a close family
- My nearest and dearest
- The children are under my feet all the time
- My brothers are like two peas in a pod
- We rub each other up the wrong way.

How do you know if something is a metaphorical statement?

- If you can put "It's like ...", or "It's as though ...", or "It's as if ..." before the expression, it is metaphorical.
- If what is being described is referring to a different aspect of a person's life, it is probably a metaphor.
- Is the person doing it in real life, or talking about doing so? If not, it is metaphorical. Many metaphors are taken from 'real life' but are still metaphorical because they are taken from one con-

text and used to refer to another. For example, "We're standing at a crossroads", can be experienced in real life when there are a number of roads ahead of some people, but in the context of a relationship the crossroads probably represents abstract choices, not physical roads, and so the expression is metaphorical.

Activity: Can you do the actions?

The following statements describe actions. Can you actually do them in real life? If so, do them!

- Put your book down
- Put someone down
- Put your coat on
- Put the kettle on
- Push a door
- Push the boundaries
- Push your limits
- Push someone to give you an answer

Notice what happens.

* * *

Sometimes a statement could be metaphorical, but you need the context to be sure. 'Put someone down' could be literal if you put down a child you had been carrying, or metaphoric if you insulted or patronised a person.

Speakers are frequently unaware that they are using metaphors; the metaphors are not carefully, consciously chosen. For example, 'the next *step*', '*give* me a *hand*', 'things are *looking up*' are all metaphors.

Here are some examples of metaphors being used spontaneously[7]:

- An executive at General Motors described his responsibilities in developing a learning environment. "The first thing I had to do was to nurture new ideas and have patience while they grew. Give them a chance to bloom."

---

[7] These examples are from Gerald Zaltman, *How Customers Think*, 2003.

- A grocery shopper complained, "I wish I could chuck the whole experience out the window."
- A parent said of his difficult child, "Dealing with him is like being on a roller coaster, except that on a roller coaster you know it's going to end soon."

We're not generally alert to metaphors in speech, and it can take some practise to become aware of them. And the more you practise, the more you will notice.

Activity: Tuning in to metaphor 1

Tune your radio to a talk station, or discreetly listen in to a conversation between two strangers, and *just listen to the words*.

Don't think about the implications of what they say, don't speculate about the backgrounds or relationships of the speakers. Just keep your ears listening to the words.

Tuning in to metaphor 2

Now give yourself a new target. Count the metaphors! As well as the 'sayings', 'commonplaces' or 'cliches', which will usually be metaphors, notice whenever someone says, "It's like …". Should you find your mind wandering, gently bring it back to the words and to the metaphors.

Tip: Almost all words that refer to space or force are metaphors e.g. 'wandering', 'gently', 'bring back'.

* * *

Did you find that the speaker seemed to use more metaphors as you continued listening? It doesn't take long to start becoming more aware of the metaphors which stand out. Then you can start to listen for those which are less obvious.

The metaphor revolution

The coins activity earlier in the chapter hints at a point of crucial importance. We easily and naturally tend to think of one thing in terms of another—that is, we think in metaphor.

The way cognitive linguists think about metaphor has been transformed in the last 25 years following the publication of George Lakoff and Mark Johnson's revolutionary book *Metaphors We Live By*. They wrote, "Our ordinary conceptual system, in terms of which we both think and act, is fundamentally metaphorical in nature."

Their conclusion that metaphor is at the foundation of the way we think is now supported by a mass of evidence across the cognitive linguistics field.[8]

It's as if we cannot think of some kinds of 'things' directly, but rather think of one thing in terms of another. We think of love in terms of warmth, for example. Time tends to be thought of in terms of space—perhaps you've put the past *behind* you, or you're looking *forward* to tomorrow?

And it's because we think in metaphor that we use so many metaphors when we talk and write: metaphoric language and metaphoric thought go hand in hand. Word choice in your native language is normally an unconscious process, and the metaphors just 'appear' among the words, without conscious thought. They tend to be fleeting and unnoticed—unless you are asked a Clean Language question or two about them.

Common metaphors

The metaphors we use in our language and our thought are far from being random. They are grounded in our embodied

---

[8] For further reading see Zoltan Kovecses, *Metaphor: A Practical Introduction*, 2002; Gilles Fauconnier and Mark Turner, *Conceptual Blending and the Mind's Hidden Complexities*, 2002; and Chapter 9 of Vyvyan Evans and Melanie Green, *Cognitive Linguistics: An Introduction*, 2006.

experience—the reality of being a person living in a body, on a planet with gravity.

In *Philosophy In The Flesh*, George Lakoff and Mark Johnson point out that the youngest baby will quickly learn that warmth means affection, love and intimacy; that important things (like parents) are big. The toddler learns to put things into containers and take them out again, and to walk towards the things he wants. All these human experiences generate a set of metaphors we can all relate to.

For example[9]:

- Affection is Warmth: "They greeted me *warmly*."
- Important is Big: "Tomorrow is a *big* day."
- More is Up: "Prices are *high*."
- Change is Motion: "My car has gone *from* bad *to* worse lately."
- Categories are Containers: "Are tomatoes *in* the fruit or vegetable section?"
- Purposes are Desired Objects: "I saw an opportunity for success and *grabbed* it."

It is clear many humans share similar metaphors especially if they share a language and culture. While we may share apparently similar underlying metaphors, the details are invariably different for each individual. Remember when we considered our individual imaginary flowers?

While every baby may begin life by learning a few common metaphors, every baby also has unique experiences. We learn about each new thing in our world and we think about it in terms of what we already know. By the time we are young children, each of us has a unique, complex network of personal metaphors reflecting our life's learning so far. By the time we are adults, a few of our personal metaphors may break through to consciousness, but the majority of the network is unconscious. Imagine the level of complexity that develops! Much as it is easy to believe that another person's metaphor is 'the same' as yours, once you examine the detail, it won't be.

---

[9] From George Lakoff and Mark Johnson, *Philosophy in the Flesh*, 1999. Also see Mark Johnson, *The Body in the Mind*, 1987.

Metaphor and Clean

By asking Clean Language questions about the metaphors a person uses, we are helping them to bring the metaphors into their awareness and to become conscious of their underlying metaphoric thought. We are providing a bridge between the parts of the mind, so that the 'hidden' is revealed.

The relationship between the conscious and unconscious has been likened to the relationship between an elephant and its rider. The rider represents the 'controlled' processes of the mind, the planning and reasoning that takes place one step at a time in conscious awareness. The elephant represents the hundreds of automatic operations we carry out every second outside of conscious awareness.[10]

In many personal development processes, the rider is taught 'tricks' by which to control their elephant. When Clean Language is used, however, the rider becomes aware of what is going on within the elephant, improves his communication with it, and finds ways to change which suit them both. This is part of what is unique to Clean Language: by enhancing communication between the conscious and unconscious it enables people to connect with their inner resources in ways that more cognitive approaches don't offer.

The relationship between elephant and rider can be a sensitive one, with people's metaphors often having deep, personal significance. If someone roughly imposes their assumptions, opinions, advice or metaphors while working with your personal metaphor, it can feel quite uncomfortable.

That's why, to get the best results while exploring a person's metaphoric world, great care needs to be taken not to 'pollute' their landscape—to stay Clean by using only the exact Clean Language questions and their own words.

❖ Eight-year-old Sam was not paying attention in class when his teacher explained new topics or gave instructions. A mentor

---

[10] Jonathan Haidt, *The Happiness Hypothesis*, 2007—thanks to Andy Smith for this reference.

helped him to become aware of his metaphor for listening well, so that he could do it more easily.

He said that to start with it was like two workmen building cogs for a machine which ran smoothly. When they were finished, they went off for their tea-break, leaving their tools on the floor. The tools caught in the turning cogs, jamming them. The mentor asked what the boy would like to have happen and he said the men needed a boss to tell them not to leave their tools lying around.

More Clean Language questions elicited information about the boss—he had a jacket and a blue cap. Then the boy said, "I haven't imagined the rest of him yet; I'll tell you next week." At their session the following week, he filled in the details about the boss: In Sam's imagination the boss came to life and set to work—the tools were no longer left scattered about, and so the cogs kept running smoothly. Sam's teacher didn't know about this metaphor work and, days later, she spontaneously told the mentor that the boy's listening had improved markedly in the preceding week. As the metaphor changed, Sam's life experience did too.

❖ A man found a 'need for speed' was dominating his life—not just in his love of fast cars but also in his work and social life. He decided it was time to 'slow down' (metaphorically) and in a 90-minute Clean Language session found his own way to do so. Clean facilitator Jane Malyon said, "There was a radical and visible change in everything about him! Before, it seemed like the frantic movements of the Keystone Cops. Afterwards, he slowed his speech, he moved with power and grace. He looked calm and thoughtful—and was too." He began to notice details like beauty in nature, shadows and light, shapes and colours— and he could hardly stop smiling. He also said if he had found this technique years ago he would never have tried drugs: it was better than any 'trip'.

❖ Coach Martin Römer from Munich, Germany, was asked by a colleague to help develop a structure for the management book he was writing. Martin explained, "After just a couple of Clean Language questions my colleague came up with a first version of his metaphor for the book's overall structure: a big red apple. As the session continued, he sorted and structured the content, honoured the overall metaphor as well as developed metaphors for sub-structures (different cuts and slices through this apple), formulated and improved the headlines of chapters and defined key style elements of the book, which had been deeply connected with the metaphor. After less than 90 minutes the session was finished, with my colleague satisfied. The metaphor gave him the basic structure for organising the book as well as a creative structure for the book's content, after months writing it one chapter at a time."

Metaphors and communication

Metaphors are important as a way of sharing our experience. Open any book, magazine or newspaper and the pages are packed with beautiful metaphors.

Metaphors in the form of stories and anecdotes are the currency of the finest public speakers; of statesmen, preachers, and teachers of all kinds; and of traditional healers and shamans. Metaphors in the form of advertisements surround us constantly, as companies seek a fast-track to our wallets. Metaphors in the form of TV shows and films keep us on the edge of our seat, laughing and crying at the director's whim.

In metaphor, information seems to come ready-packed in a way that makes it easy to pass on to others, often bypassing the conscious, critical faculties. Perhaps that's not surprising—if metaphor is central to our unconscious thinking processes, the unconscious mind may be 'tuned in' to receive information through metaphor.

Notice the impact of these fine metaphors:

- "Public opinion is the thermometer a monarch should constantly consult"—*Napoleon Bonaparte*
- "Memory is the diary that we all carry about with us"—*Oscar Wilde*

- "Words are, of course, the most powerful drug used by mankind"—*Rudyard Kipling*
- "I would rather be ashes than dust! I would rather that my spark should burn out in a brilliant blaze than it should be stifled by dry-rot. I would rather be a superb meteor, every atom of me in magnificent glow, than a sleepy and permanent planet. The function of man is to live, not to exist. I shall not waste my days trying to prolong them. I shall use my time"—*Jack London*
- "We are born princes and the civilizing process makes us frogs"—*Eric Berne*
- "In the midst of winter, I finally learned that within me there lay an invincible summer"—*Albert Camus*
- "Be like a postage stamp—stick to one thing until you get there"—*Josh Billings*

Of course, to be at all persuasive the metaphor must have some resonance in a person's experience. Anne Miller, author of *Metaphorically Selling*, gives the following example of the power of metaphor to be a "weapon of mass understanding". She quotes a salesperson describing a magazine's target audience as "the Bloomingdale's shopper and not the K-Mart lady". Readers outside the US may have to think hard (or resort to Google) to make sense of this, while American readers will instantly get the message.

And the most persuasive metaphors of all? A person's own metaphors.

Metaphors well worth sharing

Clean Language questions can be used to help someone explore the metaphors that underpin their experience so that they understand themselves better. This can be valuable in various ways, especially when they explore their particular skills and abilities. For example, if they are a creative cook but don't feel creative in other contexts, knowing their metaphor for being creative can help them to apply their creativity outside the kitchen.

It is also possible to use Clean Language to explore your metaphors of identity. As George Lakoff writes, "A large part of self-understanding is the search for appropriate personal metaphors that make sense of our lives."[11]

When you have more awareness of your personal metaphors, you may choose to share them with others. You might use your metaphor for a work skill to explain it to trainees, or share your metaphor for identity with close friends so that they get to know you at a deeper level.

❖ Celebrity chef Heston Blumenthal, known for his highly innovative cuisine, worked with Clean coach Mike Duckett to develop a metaphor for his most creative state, "Like a kid in a sweet shop". As well as helping the chef to easily access his most creative state, this metaphor was later used in 'real life' when elements such as an old-fashioned sweet shop doorbell were included in the design of his new experimental kitchen.

Consider for a moment: when *you* step into your kitchen and allow yourself to feel like a kid in a sweet shop, what happens to your creativity?

❖ Judy once used Clean Language to explore how a friend stays relaxed when she is speaking to a large audience. The friend wanted to find out how she could access that state more easily in a wider range of situations, while Judy wanted ideas to improve her own public speaking.

The friend said, "It's like being in a beautiful spring meadow. The sun's shining, the birds are singing and there's space all around me." As she talked about it and added more and more detail, her body relaxed and her face broke into a broad smile.

The friend found that, as a result, she was able to access her best public speaking state more easily, just by thinking of that meadow.

As an experiment, Judy tried thinking about a meadow as she began presentations. Of course, her meadow was different to her

---

[11] Quoted by Daniel Pink, in *A Whole New Mind*, 2006, p136.

friend's meadow. But it gave her a great starting point, and she found she became more relaxed and calm when presenting.

❖ A businessman arrived for coaching aware of all his current dissatisfactions, of what he did not want, using metaphors such as "rubbish" and "a pile of ****". His coach used Clean Language questions to help him explore his metaphor for the life he would like to experience. What emerged was a compelling image of a garden full of fascinating, colourful plants, with the client as the pottering gardener, enjoying the garden as it flourished. By developing the metaphor for what he would like, he became able to move towards it. He cleared the 'dead wood' from his calendar and began planting seeds for the future, which grew into a happier lifestyle.

The metaphors we use to describe our lives can have a profound effect on the life we actually experience. Some common metaphors include:

- Life is a game
- Life is a problem
- Life is an uphill struggle
- Life is an adventure.*

The next exercise offers an opportunity to explore a metaphor for the kind of life you would *like* to have.

Activity: Names and addresses for metaphors

Remember the "Getting names and addresses" activity in the last chapter? This time, we're going to do it using metaphor. To start with, both you and your partner need to come up with a metaphor—a metaphor for the life you would like to experience.

For example, it might be like a garden as in the story above, or like a heroic adventure, or like a three-ring circus. There is no wrong personal metaphor—whatever your metaphor, accept and value it.

---

*From Faulkner, *Metaphors of Identity*, 1991.

Compare and contrast your experience of this activity with the hobby/pastime activity in the last chapter. As speaker, what difference did it make to explore the metaphor rather than a real-life experience? As questioner, what was it like to ask about metaphor?

Begin by asking your partner, "What is your metaphor for the life you'd like to experience?" You then have a couple of minutes to find out more about it, using only the Clean Language questions:

- *(And) is there anything else about X?*
- *(And) what kind of X is that X?*
- *(And) where is X? or (And) whereabouts is X?*

and your partner's own words.

The questions can be asked several times in any order, about any aspect of the metaphor.

After two or three minutes, swap roles.

Clean Language recognises the profound significance of metaphor. The questions contain as few assumptions and metaphors as possible, so that there is space for the speaker's metaphors to grow and develop. Their inventor, David Grove, used them to help his clients to discover and explore their internal metaphoric landscapes, reach ever-deeper levels of rapport with their unconscious minds, transcend limiting beliefs and behaviours, and find resolution and healing.

In the next chapter, we'll pay attention to another important factor in his work—paying exquisite attention.

Chapter 4
Attending Exquisitely

"The quality of your attention determines the quality of other people's thinking"
—Nancy Kline

As you are learning, Clean Language questions are asked of a person's own words. So it's important to notice and recall exactly what that person says and does. Attending exquisitely is a critical step. And it needs practice.

How does conversation work?

I talk, you listen. Then you talk, I listen. Simple? Well, perhaps you think it should be.

The reality is that conversations aren't actually like that. What *really* seems to happen is more like the old joke featuring two old ladies sitting on a park bench:

First old lady, "Windy, isn't it?"

Second old lady, "No, it's Thursday."

First old lady, "So am I, let's go and have a cup of tea."

We are 'deafened' not only by age, but by a wall of assumptions and preoccupations created by what we do or do not pay attention to. It prevents us from clearly 'hearing' what another person is saying.

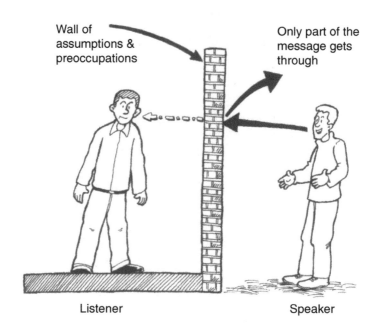

Wall of assumptions & preoccupations

Only part of the message gets through

Listener   Speaker

Expert Clean Language users seek to dismantle the wall, so they can hear the other person's message with greater clarity. With practice, you'll begin to notice more detail than the speaker is conscious of, and will be able to direct their attention so that you both find out more.

Activity: How sure are you?

Look at the picture below. Take a few moments to examine it carefully. Then write down three statements about it—things you might say to describe it to someone who can't see it.

Now score each of your statements out of 10, in terms of how certain you are that they are true (where

10 is 'certain it is completely true' and 0 is 'uncertain that it is true'). Do this before reading any further.

Taking each in turn, ask yourself, "What would have to be true for this picture to be as it is, and for my statement to be *untrue*?"

For example, you might have written the statement, "Three women are sitting on the grass in the sun", and scored it 9 out of 10 for certainty.

What would have to be true for the picture to be as it is, and for that statement to be untrue? Perhaps that the women are sitting indoors, in bright light. And are they all women?

Now, how certain are you that they are true? Finally, re-score your original statements.

* * *

Many people find that their initial certainty diminishes as they imagine more and more possible alternative scenarios outside the picture. How was it for you?

Even with a two-dimensional picture where everything is static, we make assumptions that might be inaccurate. How much more likely is it to happen in life?

Checking assumptions

We all make assumptions. Life would be all but impossible without them. And they sometimes interfere with clear communication.

You may have noticed that communication can get more difficult than normal when you are aiming to communicate with someone from:

- The opposite sex
- Another generation
- Another country

- Another ethnic group
- A very different cultural background from yourself.

Suddenly, those apparently straightforward assumptions about the way the world works have massive potential for misunderstandings. Our habitual way of thinking about things isn't always enough for communication to flourish.

It's at this point that we often feel at a loss. We don't seem to have effective tools for coping with people who have a different world view. What's needed is a respectful, sensitive way to find out what's *really* happening for the other person.

We need to become aware of our assumptions so that we can develop the flexibility to tuck them out of the way. This is not a new idea: it's the basis of many coaching approaches, negotiating strategies, and people-management theories.

Clean Language takes these approaches to their logical conclusion. It acknowledges that everyone's way of experiencing the world is different, and provides a rigorous way of finding out about alternative world views and reducing misunderstandings.

When you keep your assumptions to yourself and actively find out about the way the other person is thinking, you create space for them to think for themselves.

- ❖ In your office, how much time and money has been wasted by misunderstandings? A colleague once spent weeks producing a 20-page dossier on a particular issue when the boss had been expecting a brief email. If she had asked, "What kind of report?" at the outset she could have saved herself and the company considerable time and money.

- ❖ In your social circle, how many conversations have turned sour because someone 'took something the wrong way'? Over Christmas, a grandmother made a remark about 'young people today' which her teenage granddaughter came close to taking personally. By asking "Is there anything else about that?" the granddaughter defused the tension and enabled Grandma to be more specific. It turned out that she hadn't intended to criticise, only to observe how different things were nowadays.

Remember the 'I think we're at breaking point' example from Chapter 1? The Chair had the presence of mind not to assume this meant the point of breakdown and to ask, "What kind of breaking point is that?" "The point of breaking through," the participant said.

Notice the way the question was used to check, rather than to challenge, the assumption. Challenging assumptions can sometimes be useful—but it's wise to find out what they are.

❖ Sally was invited to a neighbour's party. "Bring a bottle and something to eat," she was told. With a busy diary she had nightmare visions of competitive cookery until she asked, "What kind of something to eat?" "Oh, could you get some olives? Mary's bringing a salad and Fred's in charge of bread." Just one Clean Language question was needed to change the amount of thought and action needed from daunting to 'manageable even on a busy day'.

The two most common Clean Language questions:

– *(And) what kind of X (is that X)?*

and

– *(And) is there anything else about X?*

are great for checking assumptions in almost any situation. Where might you find them useful?

Different realities

As you begin to notice other people's versions of reality, you'll be amazed at how varied they can be.

As we wrote this chapter we considered turning to the internet for examples of 'weird' world views—conspiracy theorists, UFO believers, train spotters and the like. And then we realised that, according to our assumptions, there were some weird views close to home.

Otherwise rational people were able to believe:

- "I must be perfect at everything."
- "Some people are just bad people and should be punished."
- "The world should be different and it's my job to change it. If I can't change it, I should worry about it."
- "I can't change my behaviour."
- "Unless I put in lots of effort, what I do has little value."
- "My life is worthless without a partner, a baby, or both."
- "I should get upset about other people's problems—and if I don't, I should feel guilty about that, because it shows that I am selfish."
- "There's only one correct way to live life—my way!"

Considered 'objectively', these are rather strange. But from the inside, as you may have experienced, your own beliefs feel absolutely true!

Activity: Noticing different realities

Here's an easy way to begin to notice other people's realities.

Tune your radio to a talk station, or discreetly listen in to a conversation between two strangers. Assume that the person *actually believes* whatever they say—that they think it's literally true.

Notice the unlikeliest things they say and wonder, "What would this person have to believe for them to honestly say that?"

For example, we overheard a woman say of her son-in-law, "He's making her life hell." For her to say that, presumably one of the things she believes is that it's possible for one person to influence another, to the extent that their life can be 'made' to be considerably different to what they would prefer. It also suggests that she believes that the influenced person is powerless to change the situation.

For another challenge, use a politician's speech. But take care—you may never listen to a politician the same way again!

Betting on realities

There are no absolutes in our knowledge of other people's realities, only safer and less safe bets. Even the things we feel very sure of, like 'the world will still be there in the morning', are not 100 per cent safe: alien attack or meteorite impact are both possibilities, if rather unlikely.

One safe assumption is that when someone says something about their experience, at some level it is true for them. And a *very* safe assumption is that you really don't know much about it.

For example, imagine that someone says, "There's something in the way of me reaching my goal." Depending on the circumstances, that could be literally true—there might be a lorry parked on their football pitch between them and the goal posts. Or they might be speaking metaphorically—the goal may be a 'life objective' and they may imagine difficulties on their metaphorical journey towards it.

In either case, the safest assumption is that even if it isn't true of their physical reality it will be true of their internal subjective experience. By asking a few Clean Language questions, you (and the other person) can find out more about it.

So a Clean conversation might begin like this. We have added comments in italics to indicate what might be the thinking behind some of the questions.

Speaker:	There's something blocking the way to my goal.
Questioner:	What kind of something?
Speaker:	A lorry, parked on the football pitch.

Or:

Speaker:	There's something blocking the way to my goal.
Questioner:	What kind of something?

Speaker:	A mountain of problems.
Questioner thinks:	*"I wonder what kind of mountain it is when it's a mountain of problems … and where is it in relation to this person and their goal?"* and then asks: What kind of mountain is that mountain of problems?
Speaker:	It is like an endlessly tall pile of big tumbled boxes like huge rocks, and it simply can't be scaled. It is like a cliff face.
Questioner thinks:	*"I wonder whether it is like that from every angle. And where is he looking at it from?"* and then asks: And when it simply can't be scaled, where are you?
Speaker:	Well, I was standing right up against it, head bent back, looking up. Now I've taken several steps back and I'm walking around the 'mountain'. It is more like a molehill from where I am now. It will be simple enough to get around it.

Realising how much you *don't* know will naturally encourage you to become curious, to find out. And because Clean Language questions are designed to include as few assumptions as possible, they are great tools for doing that in a way which feels respectful to the other person.

Curiosity with respect is a vital factor in getting those great answers from people: more specific, more truthful, more comprehensive and more interesting.

And, as you learn to trust the process and the other person learns to trust you, you can take things to a different level: asking not just for information they already know, and thoughts they know they have had, but encouraging them to search for new insights just beyond that ... then beyond that ... and beyond that ...

As you become skilful at noticing your own assumptions, and keeping them out of the way, you open the way to communicating well in difficult situations. By resisting the urge to use your own life experiences and expectations to fill in any gaps in the information you have been given, and by using just the Clean Language questions we've mentioned in this chapter, you can effortlessly transform many misunderstandings into successful interactions. As you notice your assumptions, you will also become more aware of assumptions that others are making. You can use the same two questions to help other people make sense to each other, or to alert them to their assumptions.

Managing your attention

So you're noticing more about assumptions, and developing the skill to set them aside when it's appropriate to do so.

What's next? Let's tackle the other element of that wall around us— our preoccupations. It's there in the word 'pre-occupation'—we are occupied before we even start to listen. When you aim to be a better listener, your preoccupations need to be set aside.

Where is your attention as you're reading this? If you're on public transport, at least a part of your mind will presumably be noticing the stops and waiting for your own. How much of your attention is on the people near you, and on their conversation? If you're at home, perhaps you're thinking about your next meal, or half-listening to the radio?

Activity: Tuning in

Here's an exercise to develop your listening skills. As in the last exercise you will use a radio talk station, or a conversation between two strangers, and this time, concentrate on listening to the words.

Now give yourself a new target: count the "ums" and "ahs" in two minutes. If you find your mind wandering, gently bring it back to the words, to what's being said.

And now try noticing how many times a word is repeated, or try identifying the verbs or prepositions.

Finally, aim to notice as many metaphors as you can.

You can practise this whenever you're waiting in a queue, travelling on public transport, or listening to the radio or TV.

In our fast-moving, multimedia, globalised world, we're losing the skill of doing just one thing at a time, and giving it our full attention. To use Clean Language effectively, you'll want to develop that skill.

There's a lot to be said for doing just one thing at a time, and giving it your full attention. 'Being fully present' or 'in a flow state' feels great, and is at the heart of various spiritual practices. In real life, not everyone finds it easy to do all the time. How often does anyone really listen these days?

Twelve tips to improve your listening

1. Put your attention on what the other person is actually saying rather than on the person themselves or what you think they might mean by their words.
2. 'Soft focus' your eyes to take in the whole scene, rather than looking into the eyes of the other person.
3. Give them time.
4. Set your personal agenda aside, at least temporarily.
5. Visualise: mentally create your own diagram or model of what the other person is saying but remember it is just that—*your* diagram or model, not theirs.
6. Believe what the other person is saying. Treat the words as if they are literally true for the speaker.
7. Repeat back some of their words or phrases exactly as you heard them.
8. Take notes, if appropriate, if it helps you to pay attention.
9. Know your own best listening state (see activity in Chapter 2).
10. Be curious.
11. Practise!
12. Turn your internal commentator down or off.

Many people find themselves preoccupied by the voice(s) in their heads, their 'internal dialogue', that personal commentator that has so much to say. To become a better listener, you might decide to stop talking to yourself, or at least turn down the volume! It is possible—see below.

Some ways to quieten internal dialogue

- Put your attention outside yourself.
- Some people achieve a sudden silence by physically taking hold of their tongue.
- Notice your internal dialogue and say 'sssshhhhh' to yourself.
- Place your tongue just behind your top teeth so that it's almost, but not quite, touching them.

- Imagine a ball rolling round a roulette wheel, quickly at first, and then gradually coming to a standstill.
- Put the 'real' person you are speaking to in your peripheral vision and keep your attention on what is peripheral (ignoring what is at the centre of your vision). [12]

Alternatively, you can adjust your internal dialogue to make it more helpful in focusing your attention. 'Musing' silently about what the other person is saying will help you to notice the gaps in what has been said so that you can decide what questions to ask next (see the 'Something blocking the way to my goal' transcript earlier in this chapter for an example of musing).

If you are going to ask yourself questions, some useful questions to ask are:

- What words are they emphasising?
- What words do they repeat?
- What unusual words do they use?
- Have they finished thinking or should I wait longer before asking my next question?

Checking in

Another good way to keep your attention focused on what is being said in a conversation is to repeat words or phrases, particularly those that seem important, back to the speaker.

Don't paraphrase, 'parrot-phrase'! Repeat their words exactly. Whenever you use your words rather than theirs, you're probably introducing your own assumptions, with all their potential for misunderstandings.

- ❖ Wendy recently saw a chiropractor, telling him, "My neck feels like it's not well-oiled." "Oh, you mean it's grinding?" he asked. "Well, no ..." said Wendy.

---

[12] Thanks to Reg Connolly, Jamie Smart and Eric Robbie for some of these ideas.

While Wendy could make everyday sense of the word 'grinding', the only way she could make sense of it in relation to her neck was to 'try on' grinding and compare it to her actual neck experience, and report that it did not match her experience. After learning some Clean Language basics the chiropractor began to ask questions about 'well-oiled' and 'not well-oiled', helping Wendy to focus on her experience and provide more information about the nature of it more easily.

When you repeat their words, it confirms to the other person that you really are listening, and that you've heard them correctly. For many people, this acknowledgement will be exceptional and special. Being listened to exquisitely is an increasingly rare experience.

When a person hears their words said back to them they are able to pay attention to what they are actually saying, which can be a new experience. And, often, it will encourage them to offer more information about their subject, even without a question from you. Also it can help both of you to remember what's been said.

And if the words they have said aren't quite the right ones for them, they will probably correct themselves. Actually, they might correct *you* even if you've repeated back exactly what they've said, but that's OK—in the end you'll know what they *really* meant to say.

Repeating back the other person's words exactly is one of the hallmarks of using Clean Language. We'll return to this idea, and develop it, later. But before we do, we're going to explore the rest of the basic Clean Language questions.

"A good listener is not only popular everywhere, but after a while he gets to know something"—Wilson Mizner

Chapter 5
The Developing Questions

"The greatest good you can do for another is not just to share your riches,
but to reveal to him his own"
—Benjamin Disraeli [13]

The basic Clean Language questions of David Grove

X and Y represent the person's words or non-verbal signals

Developing Questions

- *(And) what kind of X is that X?*
- *(And) is there anything else about X?*
- *(And) where is X? or (And) whereabouts is X?*
- *(And) that's X like what?*
- *(And) is there a relationship between X and Y?*
- *(And) when X, what happens to Y?*

Sequence and Source Questions

- *(And) then what happens? or (And) what happens next?*
- *(And) what happens just before X?*
- *(And) where could X come from?*

Intention Questions

- *(And) what would X like to have happen?*
- *(And) what needs to happen for X?*
- *(And) can X (happen)?*

---

[13] Quoted in James Geary's *Guide to the World's Greatest Aphorists*, 2007.

In Chapter 1 we introduced the basics of the Clean Language process.

- Listen attentively
- Remember that your assumptions, opinions and advice are your own
- Ask Clean Language questions to explore a person's words, particularly their metaphors
- Listen to the answers and then ask more Clean Language questions about what they have said.

As you now know, Clean Language questions are asked about a person's own words or non-verbal signals (indicated by 'X' and 'Y' above), and include nothing else. No "tell me about", no "please", no "would you like to"—nothing else.

The idea that you add *none* of your own words can seem limiting at first. But with practice, as you discover how effective these questions can be, following the Clean Language format will become second nature. You may also find that you experience a sense of freedom from the trouble of having to subtly alter another's words to come up with a reasonably paraphrased comment. And finally, it may be a relief not to have to construct a clever question or comment in an attempt to 'make' someone change.

In this chapter we'll start to explore the details of the questions themselves, and suggest some of the best ways to use them.

Most of the questions are quite ordinary—you probably use them every day. With others, when you add the person's words you'll notice that the wording seems a little bit unusual. While you may feel that English grammar isn't getting a look-in, the person answering them seldom notices the unusual wording. The questions have been honed over a number of years to keep the questioner's assumptions out of the way, and to maximise the information uncovered. The rule is: the less you put in, the more they will get out.

When you're learning Clean Language, it's important to use the questions in exactly their original form, since it's so easy to slip your own assumptions back into the mix. Later, you'll be able to craft your own Clean or 'Cleanish' questions from the logic of the other person's answers but, meanwhile, enjoy experimenting with this new approach in its pure form. It may be quite different to what you normally do, and that's one of the reasons it's so exciting.

Types of Clean Language questions

The twelve basic Clean Language questions (originally devised by David Grove) are normally divided into three groups:

1. The Developing Questions, which are by far the most frequently used and which include the Name and Address Questions we met earlier.
2. The Sequence and Source Questions, used to clarify the order in which things happen or where a symbol came from.
3. The Intention Questions, which tend to be most useful when Clean is being used to help a person (or group) to change in some way.

1. Developing Questions

When you use the Developing Questions, it's as if you are in an old-fashioned photographic darkroom, developing an image from what looks like a blank sheet of paper.

The Developing Questions encourage a person to be more specific, to become clear about what's true for them. It is often worth asking these questions about a single word or short phrase they have used. The Developing Questions 'stop time' by keeping attention fixed on whichever of their words you select to ask your question about.

When working in metaphor, the people or things that a person refers to are known as 'symbols', the specific details of something are its 'attributes', and symbols are arranged in a 'metaphor landscape'. But notice that all the Clean Language questions can be used to ask about 'real life' experience as well as metaphors.

Several Developing Questions asked of a single symbol or relationship will reveal more detail to elaborate and deepen their experience and to keep the symbol or relationship in the speaker's awareness.

Develop symbols with attributes, locations and relationships

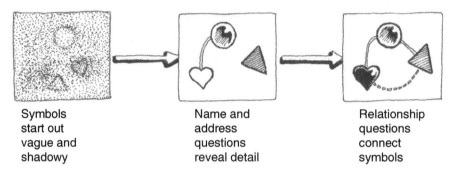

| Symbols start out vague and shadowy | Name and address questions reveal detail | Relationship questions connect symbols |

To make learning about the Developing Questions simpler, we divide them into three groups: 'name and address', 'asking for a metaphor' and 'relationship' questions.

Joe Bloggs
33 House Villas
Crown Street
Bigtown

The Name and Address Questions

You have already encountered the first three Developing Questions, the Name and Address Questions:

- *(And) what kind of X (is that X)?*
- *(And) is there anything else about X?*
- *(And) where is X? or (And) whereabouts is X?*

These questions can be asked at almost any time, about almost anything. Keep them handy!

In a recent session facilitated by Penny Tompkins, one of the most experienced Clean Language users in the world, these three questions made up two-thirds of the total questions asked. This gives a sense of how useful these three questions are.

As we saw earlier, once you have a name and address for something, you can:

- Remember it easily
- Make a quick, precise note of it
- Stay in touch with it
- Reveal connections between it and other things
- Expect the other person to remember it
- Return to it easily if you need to do so in future.

The Name and Address Questions help a person to get specific about what they are thinking and talking about. When these questions are asked about a person's metaphorical words or phrases, they help make the metaphor more tangible and bring its existence into their conscious awareness.

The Developing Questions, and the Name and Address Questions in particular, are especially useful when exploring emotions. Have you ever noticed that, when you feel an emotion, you tend to feel it somewhere in or around your body? Perhaps you haven't consciously noticed this before; usually with a little focus on how you know that you're feeling happy, jealous or calm, etc. you will become aware of the associated physical feelings. Helping someone become aware of the location of an emotion enables them to become aware of any other information that the emotion holds for them.

Example transcript: Champagne bubbles

(Clean Language questions highlighted in italics)

Questioner: When you are curious in just the way you like to be, *that is like what*?

Speaker: It is like I have a buzzy feeling and my eyes and ears open wide.

Questioner: A buzzy feeling, and *where is that* buzzy feeling?

Speaker: It is in my chest.

Questioner: *Whereabouts* in your chest *is* that buzzy feeling?

Speaker: Quite high up.

Questioner: A buzzy feeling, quite high up in your chest. *And what kind of* buzzy feeling *is that* buzzy feeling?

Speaker: Mmm ... I've been trying to work out what that feeling is ... it's a bit like popcorn popping but that isn't quite right ... No, I can't get it.

Questioner: A bit like popcorn popping but that isn't quite right. And when popcorn popping isn't quite right, *is there anything else about that* buzzy feeling?

Speaker: It's like it dances about ... Oh I know, it's like champagne bubbles in my chest!

Questioner: Champagne bubbles quite high up in your chest. *Whereabouts* quite high up are those bubbles?

Speaker: Right in the middle of me.

Questioner: Champagne bubbles quite high up in your chest, right in the middle of you. *And is there anything else about* champagne bubbles like that?

Speaker: Their popping makes me sit up and take notice.

Questioner: You sit up and take notice, *and what kind of* take notice is that?

Speaker: It's to do with opening my eyes and ears.

Questioner: Opening your eyes and ears. *And what kind of* opening *is that* opening?

Speaker: Mmm ... it is like the champagne bubbles pop them open—wide open—so that I can drink in everything that is available.

This transcript gives you a worked example of using the Name and Address Questions and shows how just using these three questions can enable someone to go beyond what they already know to access a new kind of information about themselves. It is also an example of an emotion—curiosity—being located somewhere within the body, which is where people most commonly think of their feelings as being.

Incidentally, curiosity is a very valuable attribute to have for someone using Clean Language and you might like to consider what it is like for you when *you* are curious in just the way that you like to be.

Example transcript: Super-slow motion

Questioner:	When you are listening at your best, that's like what?
Speaker:	It's like in *The Matrix* when everything slows down. Where everything goes in super-slow motion.
Questioner:	And everything goes in super-slow motion. And what kind of super-slow motion is that super-slow motion?
Speaker:	It's the kind where it's impossible to miss anything.
Questioner:	The kind where it's impossible to miss anything. And is there anything else about that impossible to miss anything?
Speaker:	It's just very simple.
Questioner:	It's just very simple. And is there anything else about that just very simple?
Speaker:	I think it's just that it's simple and very calming.
Questioner:	Simple and very calming, and whereabouts is that simple and very calming?
Speaker:	Just outside of me, just beyond my head.
Questioner:	And just outside of you, just beyond your head. And whereabouts just beyond your head?

Speaker:	Just there (*gestures about three inches behind the back of head*).
Questioner:	And whereabouts 'there'?
Speaker:	It's just behind my head, about a hand span behind my head.

This example gives you a further chance to get a sense of the process of asking Name and Address Questions, showing how you can re-ask questions, in whatever order seems useful, and that multiple where/whereabouts questions really focus on the precise location ("a hand span behind my head") where they are experiencing the sensation, in this example "calming". Notice that in this example, as happens quite often, the person has located "simple and calming" outside their body.

The 'Asking for a Metaphor' Question

Once you have identified some symbols and locations for them (some names and addresses), the speaker may spontaneously offer a metaphor, "It's like …". If not, you might want to use the Clean Language question which invites a person to come up with a metaphor:

– (And) that's X like what?

Ask this question slowly—v … e … r … y   s … l … o … w … l … y. Give the person's imagination a chance to work … and give them time to come up with an answer almost before you finish asking the question.

Notice that we ask, "And that's X like what?" rather than "And what's that like?" We want a metaphor, and the form of the question "And that's X like what?" is most likely to get one.

The chance of the person finding a metaphor is dramatically increased by asking the 'like what?' question about adjectives and other descriptions, rather than abstract concepts. For example, "That's freedom like what?" is a more difficult question for most people to answer than, "That's white, glittering and moving like what?" or, "That's strong and flexible like what?" Generally it's best to ask at least a few 'And what kind of X?' and 'And is there anything else about X?' questions to get a description of a concept before asking for a metaphor.

The 'like what?' question can also work well if you don't add the other person's words to the sentence, phrasing your question as:

— *(And) that's like what?*

Or you might ask:

— *(And) all of that's like what?*

if you would like a metaphor for all that they've been saying.

Beware of asking "That's X like what?" about something which is already a metaphor—it's not usually helpful, and can be quite annoying for the person to try to answer. For example, if you ask, "And when life is like a bowl of cherries, that's a bowl of cherries... like what?" A reasonable response to this might well be, "It's like a bowl of cherries, you idiot!"

'Relationships between Symbols' Questions

Once you have two symbols, you can find out if, and how, they relate to each other. The Clean Language questions for this are:

- *(And) is there a relationship between X and Y?*
- *(And) when X, what happens to Y?*

Finding out about the relationship between the symbols is as important as finding out about the symbols themselves—the relationship is what turns a static heap of 'stuff' into a dynamic system. But the symbols also play an important part, because you can only have a relationship if you have two or more things.

Relationships can make a profound difference. Imagine a metaphor with symbols of a man and a horse. Some possible relationships between the man and the horse would include:

- Sees
- Kicks
- Pulls
- Is on
- Distrusts
- Is under
- Approaches.

What difference would each of these relationships make to your understanding of the situation? In a number of them, either the horse or the man could be the one doing the action, which introduces still more possibilities. It makes a difference whether the man is on the horse or the horse is on the man.

Notice that we ask, "*Is* there a relationship … ?" to leave the person as free as possible to say 'no', rather than assuming that there is a relationship by asking, "*What* is the relationship …?"

Now that we've introduced all the basic Developing Questions— Name and Address, Asking for a Metaphor, and Relationship Questions—you have all you need to develop, or make three-dimensional, whatever someone is talking about. And it is the perfect time for you to start using the questions. Here is an activity for you:

Activity: Practising the Developing Questions

Each day this week, choose one of the Developing Questions and find opportunities to ask it in everyday conversation: at work, at home, on the phone, when shopping.

Once you're comfortable with asking the questions individually, try asking them several times, in any order, about various aspects of the thing under discussion.

Notice what happens.

- What kind of responses do you receive?
- Is there anything else about those responses?
- What happens for you when you ask questions in this way?
- What seems to happen for the other person?
- What happens to the relationship between the two of you?

The six Developing Questions form the heart of Clean Language. Use plenty of them, often, to encourage internal images, feelings and sounds to emerge into the light of awareness.

Now let's 'complete the set' by exploring the remaining six questions.

Chapter 6
Sequence, Source and Intention Questions

"The chain of destiny can only be grasped one link at a time"
—Winston Churchill

The basic Clean Language questions of David Grove

X and Y represent the person's words or non-verbal signals

Developing Questions

- *(And) what kind of X (is that X)?*
- *(And) is there anything else about X?*
- *(And) where is X?* or *(And) whereabouts is X?*
- *(And) that's X like what?*
- *(And) is there a relationship between X and Y?*
- *(And) when X, what happens to Y?*

Sequence and Source Questions

- *(And) then what happens?* or *(And) what happens next?*
- *(And) what happens just before X?*
- *(And) where could X come from?*

Intention Questions

- *(And) what would X like to have happen?*
- *(And) what needs to happen for X?*
- *(And) can X (happen)?*

Sequence Questions

One of the ways we structure our thinking is to break the continual flow of time into separate events. An 'event' can take a fraction of a second or millions of years—it depends who is doing the thinking and what their purpose is. Thinking of the world in terms of events allows us to focus on one piece of our experience at a time.

Whatever event the person is focusing on, there will always be something that happened before it, and something that happens after it. The Sequence Questions can help a person to tease out the details of the sequence of events. This then increases their awareness of the moments where they might have a chance to do something different in the future, or allows them to notice the signals that indicate that a situation is playing out exactly as they want it to be.

Listening to someone explain something can sometimes be like walking into a movie after it's started—you need to know about the beginning to understand the middle and the end. At other times, it's not until you get to the end that the whole plot makes sense.

For some speakers, it isn't obvious that there *is* a sequence. They may forget that the bit they are focusing on now is like just one 'frame' of a movie, and there are other frames preceding and following it. Or perhaps the person's experience is that things happen so fast that they can't work out the sequence by themselves.

❖ A client with a weight problem told Wendy, "I don't know how it happens. Each time I fill up the car with petrol, I get home with an empty ice cream wrapper." For the client to understand how this sequence kept happening and to make different choices she needed to pay attention to the many steps in between arriving at the petrol station and buying and then eating an ice cream: making a different choice means responding differently after one of the steps and before the next. By teasing out the steps, she became aware of where her response could change.

To help her do this, Wendy needed the Sequence Questions. These are designed to stretch time in ways that allow a person to find missing or unconscious information.

The Sequence Questions are:

– *(And) then what happens?* or *(And) what happens next?*
– *(And) what happens just before X?*

Notice that these questions ask about sequence: before, during and after. They are not necessarily about the past, the present and the future. They focus the person's attention on what happened before or after the thing that they are currently paying attention to. That thing could be long ago in the past, far in the future, or it could be something happening at the moment that they are being asked.

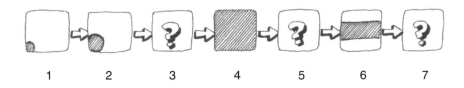

| 1 | 2 | 3 | 4 | 5 | 6 | 7 |

In this seven-step diagram, the speaker has mentioned four of the steps, but there are some steps missing in the logic of the sequence, indicated by question marks. We don't know what happens in box 3: does the circle continue to grow until its black colour fills the entire frame? Or does a large black square appear from another direction and overwhelm the circle? We don't know what happens in box 5 either: has the black colour shrunk, or been painted over? And we don't know how the story ends.

Asking Sequence Questions helps the speaker to fill in information that they may not have realised was missing.

The Sequence Questions are also used to help a person decide where an event starts and where it finishes. As a general rule, much of the action happens at the boundaries of an event—at the beginning and end. Once a habitual behaviour has started it is usually hard to stop, but catching it just before it starts gives a person the option to do something different.

Different people respond differently to the two forms of this sequence question:

– *(And) then what happens?* or *(And) what happens next?*

although they will usually themselves remain consistent in how they respond to each version. Some understand one of the questions to mean, "What happens in the very next moment?" while others will take this message from the other form of the question. So there is only one thing to do: experiment, see how the person responds, and then use the appropriate question form.

The Sequence Questions are invaluable in practically every piece of information-gathering or change work. Once you are used to them you will not want to be without them.

The Source Question

– *(And) where could X come from?*

This is one of the least-used of the basic Clean Language questions. So how does it earn its place as one of the 12? There is a good reason, 'Where could X come from?' is the one question that directs the person to find out about the origin of a symbol or attribute, etc. Often this is something that they have not considered before, and so the question frequently elicits new information.

The Source Question is rather different from most of the other basic Clean Language questions because it can generate several different kinds of 'source' information—any of which you can then ask a further question about.

For example:

"And where could that hat come from?" could generate at least five distinct kinds of information:

- Time   "From way back in the past"
- Space   "From a town in Cornwall"
- People   "From my best friend"
- Ancestry   "It's inherited from my mother's family"
- Origin   "A hat factory."

There may be other possibilities too, e.g. "from my tendency to hoard things" or "from winning it as a prize". The answer depends on what you ask the question about, and where a person considers that something has 'come from'.

The Source Question can be used to help someone find the source of a resource, such as love, energy, light, happiness, etc. When working with change, an awareness of the source of a resource is often a still greater resource for the person. Sometimes, just the awareness of having such a powerful resource can be all that they need to resolve an issue—even an issue for which their particular resource is not apparently of value. It is as though being reminded that they *have* resources is enough to change their state so that they can tap into their many other resources and access their ability to sort out issues and reach their desired outcomes.

"(And) where could X come from?" can usefully be asked repeatedly. A person rarely gets to the source of a resourceful symbol in one jump. They typically take a number of 'jumps' or 'steps' to reach the source.

You can also use this question to get a sense of perspective, or to 'un-jumble' a complex situation or experience.

In summary, the Source Question is a surprising question with a number of different kinds of answer, but it is one that has an important purpose and is worth keeping in the front of your mind so it is ready to be used when needed.

Example transcript: Clarity

In this session, the speaker wanted to find out more about how she experiences 'clarity', so that she could go into the state more easily and reliably. It provided an opportunity to use Sequence and Source Questions.

Questioner: And when clarity, what kind of clarity is that clarity?

Speaker: It's a clarity whereby there is space for multiple things but where each thing is very easy to focus in on and work with.

Questioner: A space for multiple things, but each thing is very easy to focus in on and work with. And when it's clarity like that, is there anything else about clarity?

Speaker: It's entirely transparent.

Questioner: Entirely transparent. What kind of transparent?

Speaker: A kind of transparent whereby you can look into the water and you can see a fish and you can see the sand. You can see everything.

Questioner: You can look into the water and you can see the fish and you can see the sand. You can see everything. And when you can see everything like that, is there anything else about see?

Speaker: I can hear everything also.

Questioner: You can hear everything also. And water and fish and sand, and you can hear everything also. And is there anything else about hear everything?

Speaker: Yes. I have to be grounded before I can actually hear everything.

Questioner: You have to be grounded before you can actually hear everything. And water, fish and sand, and entirely transparent, and clarity. And is there a relationship between grounded and clarity?

Speaker: Absolutely and they're actually inseparable.

Questioner: And they're inseparable. What kind of inseparable?

Speaker: Really, just that I can't get clarity without being grounded so that they are connected.

Questioner: And whereabouts is clarity?

Speaker: In my chest.

Questioner: And it's in your chest, is there anything else about it when it's in your chest?

Speaker: It's very quiet and focused.

Questioner: Very quiet and focused in your chest. And you can't get clarity without being grounded, and when you get clarity then what happens?

Speaker: It's very, very easy and very, very simple.

Questioner: Very easy and very, very simple, and what happens just before you get clarity?

Speaker: I usually breathe out, yes, like a sigh.

Questioner: Like a sigh, breathe out. And what happens just before that?

Speaker: Yes, a sort of sudden awareness that there is just the right amount of time.

Questioner: Just the right amount of time and a sudden awareness. And where could sudden awareness come from?

Speaker: It comes from the moment. It's like if I'm grounded in the moment, then I'll have all the time I need.

Questioner: If you're grounded in the moment, then you have all the time you need. And then clarity?

Speaker: Yeah.

Questioner: And is there anything else about clarity?

Speaker: There's a smile, happiness.

Questioner: Smile, happiness, and when grounded in the moment, is there anything else about grounded in the moment like that?

Speaker: Just a sort of sense that less is more.

Questioner: A sense that less is more. And where could a sense like that come from?

Speaker: It comes up through my hands and through my feet.

Questioner: It comes up through your hands and through your feet ... and grounded in the moment and clarity ... and is there anything else about clarity?

Speaker: It's like a sense of letting go of needing more clarity, in preference to being in the moment.

Questioner: To let go of needing more clarity in preference to being in the moment. And grounded, and then a sudden awareness that there is just the right amount of time, and breathe out, like a sigh, and then clarity, transparent, you can see and can hear everything, and smile, happiness, and it's very, very easy and very, very simple.

Speaker: Yeah.

Questioner: And then what happens?

Speaker: And then it just makes sense ...

In this example, notice how central the Sequence Questions are to expanding the speaker's awareness of how to get into a state of clarity. Knowing the 'name and address' of clarity is obviously valuable, but it is the exploration of the steps that lead to clarity that provide a 'route map' for getting to experience it more. The Source Question also plays an important part in making clear how a "sudden awareness" and the "sense that less is more" fit into the way she experiences clarity.

Intention Questions

These are great questions in any sort of coaching context where the person involved has a desire for something to be different, i.e. they want something to change. And questions about intention are a hallmark of Clean; asking them often generates surprising and impactful realisations.

❖ The Intention Questions were used to create a 'one-minute motivator' for leaders of weight management clubs to increase members' motivation during their weekly weigh-in.[14] Members were asked "And what would you like to have happen?", "What needs to happen for X?" and "And can X happen?" Instead of being told what to do, or being cajoled into agreeing to change a behaviour, members became skilled in setting their own weekly goals and acting on them.

The question:

– *(And) what would X like to have happen?*

normally opens a Clean Language session, with 'you' replacing 'X', "And what would you like to have happen?" Use it whenever you would like to get a person to talk about some aspect of their hopes and dreams, rather than those magnetically attractive problems we're so used to.

---

[14] See Chapter 14 for more about this project.

There are many good reasons for asking this question. One of them is that simply finding out more about our desired outcomes is often enough for us to work out how to achieve them.

Another is that talking and thinking about what you want in positive terms gets your entire system focused on that goal, rather than on all the millions of ways of doing something different. Imagine doing your weekly grocery shop with a list of all the things you *don't* want! It's much easier to shop for the more limited number of items you *do* want.

As far as the brain is concerned, the effect of mentally rehearsing an action is not very different from doing it, and thinking about what you would like to have happen can train your brain to achieve it.[15] Asking, "What would you like to have happen?" and holding a speaker's attention on the answer will encourage them to mentally rehearse their desired behaviour, so that when the time comes to put it into practice, they're ready!

So, "I want to be healthy, wealthy and in a happy relationship" works in a way that "I don't want to be poor, single or in an unhealthy relationship" does not. Equally, "I want to eat healthily and achieve my ideal weight" is more helpful than "I want to stop being so fat."

Some of the things a person is paying attention to may have desires of their own, too. These might be real-life people such as partners, parents and children, or metaphorical symbols such as 'parts of myself'. For example, a person's desired outcome might be 'to get fit' and there might be two parts of themselves—an 'athlete' who wants to go to the gym and a 'couch potato' who wants to watch TV. You can ask, "And what would athlete like to have happen?" and "And what would couch potato like to have happen?" in order to make clear the conflicting wants. In this way, the person can become aware of *both* of the wants, and this increases the chances of finding a way to get both parts on board. If they worked just with the desire of the athlete, the couch potato might well sabotage gym visits—possibly without the person realising how it came about that they were not getting fit.

---

[15] Ian Robertson, *Mind Sculpture*, 2000.

Necessary Conditions Questions

These questions explore causality and possible obstacles.

– *(And) what needs to happen for X?*
– *(And) can X (happen)?*

"And what needs to happen for X?" invites consideration of what conditions need to be in place or need to be met for a particular desired outcome to be achieved.

The question "And can X (happen)?" checks whether a desired outcome, a part of it, or a necessary condition for it, seems possible.

It's usual to ask layers of these questions, first finding out all, or most, of the conditions that need to be in place for the desired outcome to be achieved and then checking if each of the conditions can be met.

Start by asking, "And what needs to happen?" about the speaker's whole desired outcome or about one element of it, e.g. "And what needs to happen for you to experience clarity?" Then keep exploring until you have broken down each condition into components of a size and type that they can achieve. This can be done either in metaphor, or in real-world sensory information—what the person sees, hears or feels.

Once you're fairly sure a condition is achievable, then you can ask:

– *And can X (happen)?*

If the answer is 'Yes', then ask whether the next condition can be met, and the next, and the next until all are accounted for. At this point, you can ask, "What is the first thing that needs to happen?" if it seems appropriate.

If the answer to 'And can X (happen)?' turns out to be 'No', then start another layer of questioning by asking, "And what needs to happen for X?" to break the conditions down into more manageable chunks.

Don't rush to start asking these Intention Questions: it will save time in the long run to focus on asking Developing Questions and Sequence Questions first. Conditions often emerge naturally from taking this time, and may be resolved without any need for you to ask "What needs to happen?" or "And can X happen?"

❖ Climbing instructor Chris Barratt uses a Clean approach with his young clients on high ropes adventure courses. "Just as they're about to start climbing," he said, "I ask them, 'And what would you like to have happen?' I've had some great answers (some that I've never heard before) and I have followed these answers up with the other Clean questions with interesting results."

Example transcript: Conquering Everest

Picture the scene: A Clean facilitation taking place on a high ropes course during a team-building event, as a nervous climber prepares to make her move.

Questioner: And what would you like to have happen?

Speaker: Getting halfway up will be like conquering Everest for me—and I am going to do it!

Questioner: And what needs to happen for you to get halfway up?

Speaker: Volunteer to go first before I get too scared; tighten my harness so I can feel it snug around me; feel at one with all those who have made it up Everest; and imagine myself planting a flag when I get there. (*Four conditions.*)

You will notice that her first two conditions (volunteering and tightening her harness) are real-world based and the last two are metaphoric. We treat them both in the same way.

Questioner: And what needs to happen for you to volunteer first? (*Addressing the first of the four conditions.*)

Speaker: I need to stand at the base of the pole, tell everyone that I am going first so I can't back out when the instructor asks, and keep moving so that my legs don't turn to jelly with fear. (*Three sub-conditions.*)

Questioner: And can you stand at the base of the pole? (*Addressing the first sub-condition; fairly sure she can do it, therefore the 'And can …' question rather than 'And what needs to happen for you to stand at the base of the pole?'*)

Speaker: Yes. I'll go there now before anyone else gets there.

Questioner: And can you tell everyone that you are going first? (*Addressing the second sub-condition.*)

Speaker: Yes. Listen everyone—I'm climbing this pole first!

The facilitator carries on questioning until the three sub-conditions and the tightening harness condition are met. Fast-forward to:

Questioner: And what needs to happen for you to feel at one with all those who have made it up Everest?

Speaker: I need to believe I can do it.

Questioner: Is there anything else that needs to happen?

Speaker: No. That's it.

Questioner: And can you believe you can do it? (*Taking a chance here—not certain if she does believe it.*)

Speaker: I'm not sure. It is a long way up. I am scared of heights even if they aren't very high, you see. (*Proof that it was too big a jump to ask 'And can you?' here.*)

Questioner: And what needs to happen for you to believe that you can do it? (*Go back to breaking this condition down into smaller 'bits'.*)

Speaker: Well, remember that I am strong; that the colleague holding my rope is a fantastic person and would never let go; and that people with significant disabilities make it all the way up Everest, so I must be able to climb this pole. (*Three sub-conditions.*)

Questioner: And can you remember that you are strong?

Speaker: Yes.

Questioner: And can you remember that the colleague holding your rope is a fantastic person and would never let go?

Speaker: Yes.

There was no time for more questions as the speaker was ready to climb—right now!

She climbed well beyond her goal, to loud applause from all on the ground. She came down beaming and was noticeably more confident.

The 12 basic Clean Language questions and their purposes

The following table summarises the kind of information requested by each question:

• *(And) what kind of X (is that X)?*	Attributes
• *(And) is there anything else about X?*	Attributes
• *(And) where is X? or (And) whereabouts is X?*	Location
• *(And) that's X like what?*	Metaphor
• *(And) is there a relationship between X and Y?*	Relationship
• *(And) when X, what happens to Y?*	Relationship
• *(And) then what happens? or (And) what happens next?*	Sequence
• *(And) what happens just before X?*	Sequence
• *(And) where could X come from?*	Source
• *(And) what would X like to have happen?*	Intention
• *(And) what needs to happen for X?*	Necessary conditions
• *(And) can X (happen)?*	Necessary conditions

These 12 questions are all you need to start practising Clean Language. And remember:

- Listen attentively.
- Remember that your assumptions, opinions and advice are your own.
- Ask Clean Language questions to explore a person's words, particularly their metaphor.
- Listen to the answers and then ask more Clean Language questions about what they have said.

As a general principle, ask your Clean Language questions about the positive stuff in the speaker's landscape—the resources they have, and the outcomes they desire. Just helping a person to realise they have resources is often enough to change their relationship to a problem.

And remember to ask where a resource comes from since this often leads to an even greater resource. There are often resources within, beyond and behind other resources.

That said, there are no 'wrong questions' in Clean Language, only more or less useful ones in terms of the kind of information they generate. If a question you ask seems to lead nowhere, simply note that and move on to the next question. And because Clean Language questions contain so few assumptions, any misunderstandings on your part aren't obvious! This kind of 'no fault' questioning can be very liberating for Clean Language questioners and speakers alike. It enables you as questioner to move easily and naturalistically with the speaker's 'flow'.

As you do the following activity, keep the summary above in mind to make the most of what you have learnt so far.

The basic 12 Clean Language questions are very simple to learn. Once you know them by heart you will be able to use them easily and naturally whenever an opportunity arises, without needing to prepare in advance.

Activity: Random Clean Language questions

In this activity, you'll experiment with most of the Clean Language questions.

Make or buy* a set of cards, with a different Clean question on each one.

You and your partner each need to choose something you do well—such as cooking a meal, playing a game, being patient, etc. The first question of the activity will be the ordinary question, "What is something you do well?"

Shuffle the pack of cards and draw random Clean Language questions to ask your partner. All you need to decide is which of your partner's words to use to replace 'X' in each question. Be guided by your instinct and if a word or phrase seems like a potential resource, ask some questions about it. Both you and your partner may be pleasantly surprised.

After about 15 minutes, swap roles.

If you discuss the process afterwards, ask your practice partner how the experience was for them *before* making any comment from your own point of view as questioner. Keep your comments as Clean as possible, by only saying what you learned about asking and being asked Clean Language questions.

As questioner:
● Were some questions easier to ask? If so, do you and your partner both find the same questions easily?
● What happens to your attention when you don't have to decide which question to ask?

As speaker:
Did the questions seem random, or did they keep you exploring your experiences?

*Available from http://www.cleanchange.co.uk

Chapter 7
Modelling Cleanly

"The true voyage of discovery lies not in seeking new landscapes,
but in having new eyes"
—Marcel Proust

A person who is asked Clean Language questions about their metaphors will explore and find out about their inner world, often making surprising discoveries. It can seem as if all the action is on the inside and, for some people, this in itself is a revelation.

As the Clean Language questioner is keeping their advice and assumptions to themselves while asking Clean Language questions, is there anything else they are doing?

While asking random Clean Language questions can be surprisingly useful, the key to excellence in Clean facilitation is modelling.

What is modelling?

At its simplest, modelling is about noticing how other people do things and, if it's useful, copying them. It's something that people, children in particular, do quite naturally.

For example, Wendy recently watched her young nephew modelling his father building sandcastles. The child watched closely as the line of castles grew longer and then tried to build one for himself. He matched every move his father had made, right down to the last pat of the shovel.

As well as being a key to effective Clean facilitation, modelling is a 'life skill' with a number of applications elsewhere. It can help you to:

- Understand another person and how they do things
- Learn new skills and adopt 'best practice'
- Develop new approaches to teaching and learning
- Develop your understanding of yourself and how you do things
- Help other people discover more about themselves and, if they choose, to change.

As the questioner gives the speaker their full attention, and listens to their actual words, they are building their own mental 'diagram' of what the person is saying. In the jargon, this diagram is called a 'model' and the process of constructing it, 'modelling'. By creating their own model, the questioner is able to imagine how the pieces of information fit together for the speaker and can therefore ask targeted questions to help them fill in crucial details. Also, when the questioner models, it encourages the speaker to self-model, which is an important part of the process. This means that each person is building their own model of the speaker's experience, usually in metaphoric form.

You will have modelled someone's behaviour when:

- You have a good sense that a particular film or book will appeal to a friend
- You can guess what a colleague's reaction will be in a situation
- You can predict what your partner will order from an unfamiliar menu.

Here is another example of modelling.

❖ Over the years, a daughter modelled how her mother prepared the Christmas Day feast, because she was not allowed to help. Each dish was prepared in exactly the same way each year, and each went in at the proper time. So when the daughter got married, she was all set to recreate the occasion for her own family. But being a modern woman, her husband and visitors would be helping, of course! On the day, though, several dishes were slightly over- or under-done.

The following year, she took her new family to visit her mother, who still wouldn't let her help. She discovered what had been the crucial, missing piece of her model. Mum explained, "I have a list of what needs to be done when, and as long as I stick to it, everything will be ready on time. Having someone else doing things will always change things slightly and I don't want that because it could have knock-on effects."

The daughter's initial modelling attempts had not been comprehensive enough for her to get the same results as her mother, as she had overlooked the importance of preparing the meal by herself. But after discovering that missing piece she could use her updated model of her mother's skill so that she *could* take it on for herself, if she chose.

In both the sandcastle and Christmas dinner examples, the nephew and the daughter learned a new skill, but the father and the mother probably didn't learn much. That's a key difference between modelling someone's behaviour and modelling their internal perceptual processes, as Clean Language allows you to do. For example, using Clean Language allows you to model how someone remains hopeful, or how they maintain a sense of humour, and both you and they will probably discover new information.

How to model Cleanly

You've already done some modelling using Clean Language questions—for example, when you asked someone to think of a flower, and then asked, "What kind of flower is that flower?" If hearing their answer caused you to think of a flower more like the one they described, then you were modelling. And when you thought of that flower, where did you think of it? Was it in front of you or in front of them, at waist height or ground level or somewhere else entirely? That's where you were constructing your model in that moment.

Remember that you didn't imagine *their* flower. You imagined a flower which was something like the one they described. If you had asked more Clean Language questions to get more detail, you'd soon discover differences between their flower and the one you imagined, and then you could have adjusted your version so that it more closely resembled their version.

Just as it's easy to make assumptions and to give advice, it's very easy to forget that your model is made up of your thoughts about the speaker's words. Beware of treating your diagram or picture as if it were 'true'. It isn't—it can only ever be a rough approximation of what they're thinking. So hold your model lightly, and be ready to amend it the moment you see or hear something that tells you it's wrong, incomplete or needs updating to take account of what they have said.

Keep checking that your model is as accurate as possible and update it with all the relevant new information each time the speaker answers a question.

It's a good idea to get into the habit of first constructing your model of another person's thoughts outside yourself, as if you are an observer of it, rather than as if it is a part of you.

This is so for a number of reasons:

- To distinguish the information that you have actually heard from what you have imagined, and what you think and feel about it.
- To make it easier to keep in mind the various items mentioned, to notice relationships between them and to spot gaps in the information you have.
- To keep outside the content so you have the bigger picture and can choose your questions with that in mind.
- To minimise the possible discomfort of 'stepping into the shoes' of someone who is having a difficult time.

As a general rule, people using Clean Language build their model *around the person they are modelling*, placing the symbols wherever the speaker has referred to them as being. Once you have a more or less complete model, and if it seems appropriate, you can then decide to 'try it on', that is, step into the model you have built by putting yourself in the speaker's shoes.

Activity: Building a model

Turn on a radio talk station or TV chat show for a few minutes and listen to someone describing a fun, exciting experience. Begin to create a model of what it was like for them.

As you do this, notice *where* you build your model.

Do you construct it as if you are imagining what they saw through their eyes and feeling something of what they felt?

Or is your model somewhere outside you? For example, you might:

- Picture them having the experience, as if on a TV screen
- Construct it in three dimensions
- Have a 'work space' in front of you in which you build your model.

* * *

If you choose to, you can experiment with changing where (and how) you create your model. But the point of this activity is for you to start to model how you model. This will put you in a good position to keep learning more about how you can model at your best as you become more experienced.

Benefits of modelling using Clean Language and metaphor

Benefits to modelling subject (the speaker)

- Learns more about own process and therefore can access it more readily.
- Has a developed metaphor which can be used to teach others or used in marketing and other materials.
- Has increased choice about when to behave in line with their metaphor.
- Can lead to change if that is what is wanted.

Benefits to modeller (the questioner)	• Learns about something new.
	• Can adopt subject's approach for themselves.
	• Has a developed metaphor which can be used to teach or explain to others.

Applications of modelling Cleanly

You can use Clean Language questions to model for a number of purposes.

One of these is to find out how someone does something really well. Remember the celebrity chef in Chapter 3, who was 'like a kid in a sweet shop' as he experimented with possibilities? In Chapter 15 you'll read the story of how Judy and some colleagues modelled a firm's top-performing salesmen, and how a metaphoric superhero, Wildlife Man, emerged.

By modelling, the questioner learns something new which can be useful in all kinds of contexts. A journalist might use this approach in an interview with a celebrity or a technical specialist, or a business might use modelling to spread top performers' 'best practice' to other staff. As a by-product, the speaker will normally get new insights into how they do what they do. "I didn't know I did that!" is a comment we often hear.

❖ Coach Zannie Rose used Clean Language and facilitated a client to resolve her backache 'accidentally'. Zannie explained, "She had come about something else entirely, and she mentioned that in a particular kind of conversation it was as if she was 'being beaten with a rod'. A couple of questions later she realised that the rod beating her was like her recurrent backache, which in turn was like a rod in her back. We modelled that using Clean Language for a while and she suddenly said, 'Oh, it doesn't hurt any more!' The look on her face was priceless!"

In this example, it is clear that a client achieved a change that wasn't a conscious desired outcome in her mind, simply by being asked Clean Language questions that enabled her to self-model her experience. It is quite common for a person to reach an insight that leads to a desired change when all they started off doing was modelling their current experience of something.

❖ A client of Judy's explored his spiritual side in a Clean session. "You wake up in a strange place—you're not in Kansas any more. And slowly through that process of waking up and looking around, you realise that actually there is so much to see and enjoy and feel connected … connected like … the shape of a tornado; it's quite narrow and then it just goes up and up, making an enormous system that envelops the sky. It's a tornado of light and energy; it's both substantial and insubstantial at the same time and just goes to wherever it goes …"

We don't know whether this exploration led to the client changing his behaviour but, typically, an exploration like this results at least in the person having a greater appreciation of life.

❖ James and Penny modelled David Grove when they wanted to find out how it was that he was such an excellent therapist. They wanted to create a model they could use and pass it on to others. One way they did this was in the form of a book.[16] Their model is a process that uses a combination of Clean Language questions, metaphor and modelling, which they call 'Symbolic Modelling'.

Modelling is just as vital when Clean Language is used in change situations—for example, in coaching, consulting or therapy—as when it is used to model someone's excellence in a given skill. We'll come back to this point later in the book.

"I didn't know I did that!"

A piece of modelling using Clean Language may be done primarily for the benefit of the questioner (e.g. as a researcher) or for the benefit of the speaker who wants to find out more about how they

---

[16] James Lawley and Penny Tompkins, *Metaphors in Mind: Transformation Through Symbolic Modelling*, 2000.

do what they do. Whatever the main intention, the process will typically also result in the speaker discovering new information about themselves. This is because the speaker is also modelling—self-modelling.

The Clean Language questions naturally encourage the speaker to self-model, and to report back on the self-modelling process in answer to the questions.

❖ Judy's coaching client, Catherine, was working on her career development plan. At the start of the session Catherine was aware of having lots of options. She knew that, previously, she had successfully 'just known what choice to make', but didn't know consciously how she had done this. Judy helped Catherine to self-model by asking her Clean Language questions. At the end of the session Catherine had a metaphor of smooth, flat stepping stones stretching across a tranquil stream. She had a detailed plan for stepping to the next stone, some idea about the one after that—and no need to have a plan for the remainder. She was delighted with this metaphor.

Self-modelling is different from the modelling done by the questioner. The questioner builds up a model from what the speaker says and does in the room, with the aim of working out the logic in the speaker's information that means that things are as they are.

In contrast, the speaker is modelling their own experience, which starts out with the whole story of their life all 'joined up', and they aim to tease it apart to become more aware of how they are structuring their experience.

This awareness sets the stage for him to:

● Make best use of his skills and abilities.
● Learn and have insights about himself.
● Explore new opportunities and possibilities.
● Change in a way that works well for him.

One way that you can tell that the speaker is self-modelling is if they make a comment like, "Oh—I'm doing it again!" as they catch themselves doing one of their patterns while you are together.

Probably the only way to experience self-modelling like this is to be facilitated using Clean Language. We highly recommend that you find an opportunity to work with an experienced Clean Language user as it will deepen your appreciation of the process and help you to understand the experience of those you Cleanly question.

In summary, modelling is at the core of Clean Language because it greatly facilitates understanding, communication and the possibility of growth and change. You are already modelling in your everyday life, perhaps without being aware of it. To get really good at doing it deliberately, keep practising!

Chapter 8
Transforming Metaphors

"First comes thought; then organization of that thought into ideas and plans; then transformation of those plans into reality. The beginning, as you will observe, is in your imagination"
—Napoleon Hill

So, how do we use Clean Language questions with metaphor to help people to make the changes they would like? In this chapter and the next, we'll outline the process. Later in the book we'll provide opportunities for you to practise on yourself, before you move on to helping other people.

From here on, we'll assume you are interested in using Clean Language to help someone change something about themselves and their situation, and so we'll use the word 'client' to denote the speaker and 'facilitator' for the questioner. Please feel free to substitute terms which work better for you: for example client/coach, patient/doctor, student/teacher, direct report/manager or friend/myself.

As we mentioned in Chapter 1, the Clean Language process is fundamentally the same whether you are:

- Gathering information for your own benefit
- Gathering information for someone else's benefit (e.g. as a researcher)
- Helping another person to become clear about something or to understand themselves
- Helping another person to make a change in their life.

But before exploring someone's metaphors with a view to them making a change, it is important for there to be an agreement for you to do this, or a shared intention, that makes this appropriate. Don't just 'dive in'! Also, be sure to work only at a level that fits your experience and competence.

And remember that when using Clean Language, it's not the facilitator's job to *make* change happen. Any change that occurs comes from within the client and happens at the client's own pace, with the result that it fits them perfectly.

If change is what a person would like, then frequently that's what will happen, quite spontaneously. Just keep asking questions, listening to the answers, and helping the client to build up their model of their own experience. No special 'change technique' is required.

❖ 13-year-old Nick was in danger of being expelled from school because of his constant classroom explosions and playground fights. He wanted the teachers to 'get off his case' so he could have a quiet life. Nick's experience was as if he was surrounded by a pack of unpredictable large dogs with sharp teeth, whose job it was to protect him, and who frequently lashed out inappropriately.

His coach helped him to discover this metaphor, and then asked Clean Language questions about it and about what Nick would like to have happen instead. She listened carefully and non-judgementally to the answers, giving him time and space to develop his own thinking.

Nick liked the dogs and enjoyed the protection they gave him, but he decided that he would like to have more control of them. Over the course of a few sessions his metaphor changed: the dogs were less unpredictable and eventually he was able to order them to go to their kennel and expect to be obeyed.

In parallel, his classroom and playground behaviour transformed—he had more control of his temper and could choose to calmly disagree with others, rather than explode. In turn his teachers no longer felt a need to stay 'on his case'.

❖ A client began a session wanting to know how he could lead his team well. He started hesitantly with a metaphor of a butterfly flitting between flowers. As the exploration continued, the metaphor changed to that of a large bird. It flew high above the team, able to see the surrounding terrain and to drop down and lead the smaller birds in the direction that was needed. Finally a further change happened when he saw himself becoming a supersonic jet, able to do all that he could do before, but with increased acceleration, power and speed. It took his team a while to get used to his new approach, but once they did, they appreciated his new leadership qualities and the team's functioning improved considerably.

These examples demonstrate changes happening within a client's metaphor landscape which translate into changes in the real world, because the structure of their metaphor landscape and their real-world experience are similar. Once one changes, the other frequently follows suit.

Metaphors often change very easily. After all, however real they may seem, at one level they are simply in a person's imagination, where anything is possible. Individual symbols may also have attributes which give them the ability to make particular changes— plants can grow, birds can fly, moons can wax and wane. On the other hand, some metaphors are central to who a person is and they will resist any attempt to change them. That's one reason that it's not up to the Clean Language facilitator to try to change another person's metaphors.

The Clean Change Process

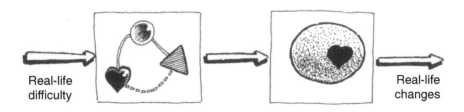

Real-life difficulty

Real-life changes

Metaphoric landscape changes

Until you've experienced it, the idea of a change in metaphor leading to a real-life change can seem surprising. But when people describe having changed they very often use a metaphor, "I got a new perspective", "I took the leap", "I let go of the hurt", etc. In Clean Language, a change in metaphor and a change in real life very frequently go hand in hand.

❖ A woman's illness was her metaphoric enemy in battle, but it became her 'best friend' as she discovered that it had brought many wonderful experiences into her life. Her attitude to the illness was transformed.

❖ Random shapes scattered around a confused, uncertain man's landscape formed themselves into a staircase, which became a real-life plan to launch his business.

❖ The 'monsters' in a man's landscape became supportive friends allowing him to relax when speaking to big groups, which had been his real-life bugbear.

❖ The metaphoric barbed-wire coils surrounding an anxious woman became a colourful 'slinky' spring toy. With this she gained a new, more helpful perspective, so she was able to go along with others' suggestions rather than needing to be constantly in control.

These examples are instances where the process continued until the metaphor itself transformed. At other times, the new knowledge will trigger an insight or 'ah-ha!', and the client will discover how to change their behaviour. However it happens, once a change occurs as a result of the process, the client will never be quite the same again.

How to facilitate change Cleanly

When using Clean Language to facilitate change, stick with the basics:

- Listen attentively
- Remember that your assumptions, opinions and advice are your own
- Ask Clean Language questions to explore a person's words, particularly their metaphors
- Listen to the answers and then ask more Clean Language questions about what they have said.

In addition to the basics, here are some ways of using Clean Language to make change more likely to occur.

When you notice a metaphor in someone's language or gestures, *treat it as if it was real* and ask Clean Language questions about it. For example, if the speaker says, with a sigh and a shake of their head, "My relationship is at a crossroads," notice that they have used a metaphor. Somewhere in their thinking there's a crossroads, and their relationship is at it.

Your natural tendency may be to ask about the 'relationship' but if you ask about the metaphor, "What kind of crossroads?" they will access completely different information.

You can also ask, "And when your relationship is at a crossroads, what would you like to have happen?" This question invites them to move their attention off the problem and onto what they would like instead, ready for you to help them develop a metaphor for what they would like.

As your questions help the client develop a metaphor for what they would like, it's possible that the metaphor may 'come to life' and become more real for them. Then information they simply weren't aware of at the start of the conversation becomes available, they will get a more strongly felt sense of their desired outcome and the learning that this offers makes it easier for them to make a change in real life.

But what if you're not yet spotting metaphors easily? Relax! They're like London buses—if you miss one, there'll be another along in a minute. In fact, studies show there'll be another six along in the next minute, on average (metaphors, that is—not buses).

Because Clean Language questions are wonderfully flexible:

- If you think you've just spotted a metaphor, you can treat it as if it was real and ask a Clean Language question about it.
- If you're not sure if it was a metaphor or not, you can assume that it was and ask a Clean Language question about it.
- If it definitely wasn't a metaphor, in other words it was sensory or abstract information, you can still ask a Clean Language question about it.

It may take practice before you regularly become aware of metaphors quickly enough to ask about them. Sometimes, the client will volunteer a fully-fledged, all-singing-all-dancing metaphor, perhaps starting with the words "It's like …", but more often the metaphor will take shape gradually. Your role then is to ask more Clean Language questions to help the picture emerge. Bear in mind that there will be hidden metaphors in the words you usually ignore in everyday conversations, such as prepositions.

What if you usually spot metaphors but the particular person you are working with seems reluctant to 'go into metaphor'? That's a cue for you to *listen even more exquisitely*.

Some suggestions for clients who tend to talk more conceptually:

- Look out for a mention of a sensation or feeling, which can also be a metaphor.
- Ask about verbs and prepositions (which are nearly always metaphoric) rather than nouns.
- Say as little as possible, encouraging them to say more on the topic.
- Just be patient. Sooner or later they are going to want to describe something complex, internal or significant for them, and will spontaneously use a metaphor.
- Use the Clean Language question:

  – *(And) that's X like what?*

This question asks the client directly for a metaphor. But it's best not to rush this question: it's used most effectively at the end of a sequence of Developing Questions which have helped the client get a fuller idea of the subject.

❖ Here's an example of how the 'like what?' question works.

One of Wendy's coaching clients was relatively new to managing client accounts. He was an excellent project manager and very task-focused. He was unconvinced about the need to attend particularly carefully to relationships in his new job. He said, "I was good at my previous job and I'm angry that my manager now evaluates me as mediocre. I want to be in the 'High Achiever' category by my next annual appraisal."

Wendy asked him about the abstract concept 'High Achiever category' using Clean Language questions and he responded with more abstract statements about how he had to convince his manager that he had the most important competency needed for the job: relationship skills.

Wendy asked, "And what kind of relationship skills are those relationship skills?"

The client answered, "Well, they consist of insubstantial talk, being enthusiastic, acting like the person is more important than the job."

Wendy asked, "And when insubstantial talk, being enthusiastic, acting like the person is more important than the job, all that is … like … what?" He paused a moment and said, "It's like I need to throw a rope across the river to where my clients are."

Notice the way that the 'Like what?' question was used:

First Wendy asked about the concept—in this case, 'relationship skills'. 'What kind of X (is that X)?' or 'And is there anything else about X?' are a good choice for this step in the process.

Then she repeated what had been said about the 'relationship skills—insubstantial talk', etc—and used these words to form the 'X' in her 'Like what?' question. This maximises the chances of the client reaching a metaphor—'throwing a rope across the river'.

Using this metaphor he discovered how he wanted to build work relationships; making sure the rope was securely anchored on the shore, asking for help to anchor it on the other side, weaving more ropes together to make it stronger.

As he explored his metaphor and worked out the steps involved in building a bridge, so the actions that he needed to take in the real world became clear to him. They had a similar structure to the bridge-building process.

While he hadn't been able to work out what to do in real life directly (it was all too complex, unknown and filled with emotion) by using metaphor he was able to make what he wanted more tangible and more contained, so he could work out how to achieve it. He applied his knowledge and, as a result, was retained by the company at a time when many people around him lost their jobs.

A common way to encourage change Cleanly, once the metaphoric landscape has been developed, is to use the question, 'What needs to happen for X?' in a systematic way, as we described in Chapter 6. But don't rush into this. Instead, take your time asking questions to enable the client to develop a metaphor for what they would like and give it time and space to transform itself spontaneously into their current reality.

In our trainings, we teach a number of ways to use Clean Language questions which make change more likely to occur (for example, the 'Seven Approaches' and the 'Framework for Change' of Penny Tompkins and James Lawley). But even the most sophisticated Clean Language users get their results by listening exquisitely, staying Clean and asking more Clean Language questions, rather than trying to force or trick the client to change. That just doesn't work!

Some important points about change

- Just because a client comes to you with a desired outcome doesn't mean that they are necessarily ready to make a change.
- It isn't your responsibility, or your right, to make a change happen for the client. It's theirs.
- You can provide opportunities for a client to have insights and new perspectives that will increase the chances of them making a change.
- Self-delusion, self-denial and self-deception and other double-binds may block a client's attempts at change. They can stop the client from being able to say what they want, prevent them from having access to parts of their metaphoric landscape, block them from knowing what conditions need to be in place or how to achieve them, or stop them from making or maintaining the change in real life. In such cases, work on the self-delusion or double-binding pattern may be needed before proceeding to

work on the desired outcome. This generally requires skilled facilitation, outside the remit of this book. However, double-binds are the exception rather than the rule and this book contains what you need for most situations.[17]

In summary, then, the Clean change process is exquisitely simple: ask Clean Language questions to develop a metaphor for what the client would like, and keep going until things change. A change within the metaphor often means that real-life change happens for the client.

In Chapter 9, we explore what happens next: the process of 'maturing' changes.

---

[17] For more about binds, see James Lawley's article, 'Modelling the Structure of Binds and Double Binds': http://www.cleanlanguage.co.uk/articles/10/1Modelling-the-Structure-of-Binds-and-Double-Binds/Page 1.html

Chapter 9
Maturing Changes

*"Imagination is the beginning of creation. You imagine
what you desire, you will what you imagine and at last
you create what you will."*
—George Bernard Shaw

So, you've developed a metaphor landscape and something has
changed. Now what?

A new change is often like a small seedling. It can be easily blown
over or trodden on. By 'maturing' that change, you grow it into a
larger, thriving plant that can withstand adverse winds and careless
or well-meaning people.

Once a change has happened, the role of the facilitator is to help the
client to continue self-modelling and develop the landscape so that
changes are deepened, extended and consolidated. Then the
changes will be more likely to stay in place when the client returns
to their original real-life context. In real life, old triggers will initially set off the client's old habits and patterns, and the expectation
of others will be that the client will do what they have always done
in the past. A well-matured change will be strong enough to withstand all of this.

In some cases, the change in the metaphor will result directly in the real-life change the client wanted. At other times, the change may be an updating of the client's desired outcome, which in turn is a step towards achieving it. In either case, take the time to nurture the seedling.

❖ Early in a Clean session, it seemed the client had the change she wanted. "The fog has cleared! I can see a clear path to my goal and all I have to do is keep walking." Her facilitator began to mature the change, asking her questions which explored the clear path and the details of the next steps on the metaphorical journey.

   She discovered that the path, which had seemed from a distance to have flowering shrubs only growing along its edges, was in fact overgrown in places, making it difficult to follow. She also realised that it would be easy to get lured into marvelling at the beauty of the various shrubs when she came upon them, and that this could lead to her wandering right off the path without realising it.

   As the maturing process continued, she discovered benches at intervals along the path, where she could sit and admire the flowers but also notice how far she had come and consider the nature of the path ahead of her and its challenges. With this awareness she was able to formulate a concrete plan of real-life action which included regular time in her schedule for briefly exploring interesting ideas that came her way, and for taking stock of where she had come from and where she was going to each time she took a break. She ended the session able to start actioning her plan straight away.

If the facilitator had concluded that nothing more was needed when the client said that the fog had cleared and she could see the path, a number of potential hazards would have remained, making it difficult for the client to stay on her path (e.g. a tendency to focus too intently on a small detail of her work, or to completely lose her goal-focus when something new and interesting occurred to her). The maturing process gave the client the opportunity to become aware of the possible difficulties she faced and, with the appearance of benches along the path in the metaphor, she could work out a real-life strategy for handling the difficulties. This made her action plan stronger and more likely to withstand the pressures of day-to-day life.

How to mature changes

Whenever you think you notice a change within the metaphor, switch your focus to 'maturing' it by asking Clean Language questions about the change, rather than about the original metaphor.

The Clean Language questions that you will use in maturing a change are the familiar ones:

- *(And) what kind of X (is that X)?*
- *(And) is there anything else about X?*
- *(And) where is X?* or *(And) whereabouts is X?*
- *(And) that's X like what?*
- *(And) is there a relationship between X and Y?*
- *(And) when X, what happens to Y?*
- *(And) then what happens?*
- *(And) what happens next?*

Specifically, use these questions to keep modelling, and ask about:

- The change itself
- The effects of the change over time
- The effects of the change on other symbols, including the client themselves.

And if anything the client says or does suggests that the change may mean that they have updated their desired outcome, ask, "And what would you like to have happen now?" before you continue developing.

Here is an example to give you a sense of maturing changes.

❖ A client faced a medical procedure to check on a troubling growth on one of her organs, and came for her session concerned about how she would handle the news of the existence of a growth over the coming eight weeks or so, while she waited for the medical investigation that would provide a diagnosis. Her desired outcome was that she wanted to "be free, fundamentally me, with energy coming from my body".

During the session she explored a feeling of floating in the pool with the sun shining down upon her and entering her through her fingers, moving through various organs and then releasing. She found that she was experiencing the feeling of being free, and she (metaphorically) emerged from the pool into a forested glade, with sun shining through the leaves. As this change was matured, the metaphor evolved to one of "coming home to myself" and it was clear she was experiencing it as she relaxed back in her seat, sighed and said, "Oh, I'd forgotten this feeling—it's been so long since I was at home to myself. It feels wonderful to come home to myself."

To mature this changed metaphor, the facilitator asked her:

- About the change:
  - Anything else about coming home like that?
  - What kind of home?
  - Where is that home?
  - What kind of I is that I that's come home? etc.

- About the effects of the change on other symbols:
  - When coming home to yourself, then what happens to energy coming from your body?
  - When coming home to a thatched cottage in the forest, surrounded by quiet and greenery, and your husband is there to greet you, and your brothers and sisters, all making you feel welcome and loved, and you love all of them, then what happens to being free? etc.

- About the effects of the change over time:
  - When all of that, then what happens?

Some time after the session the client said that with this metaphor she had gone beyond the diseased part, to another stage in life and was no longer feeling inhibited. Her creativity had returned and she could be joyous and "wholly me". Her husband had noticed the difference and was himself affected by it: he became less anxious about the medical appointment and better able to support her.

The client resigned from a job which had been weighing her down for a long time, found a job she enjoyed and had started to paint again after a break of many years. She found herself laughing more readily and had such increased energy that she began going for long walks.

When maturing a change, it is tempting to keep asking about the time following the change: what happens next, and next and next, without pausing to develop the symbols and check the effects on other symbols. This approach sometimes results in a new landscape that is very 'flat', lacking detail, which may not be as robust as it could have been if more Developing Questions had been interspersed in the maturing process. So, keep on collecting names, addresses and relationships, just as you did when developing the original desired outcome landscape.

It could be that, while a change is worth maturing, the maturing process doesn't lead to the client achieving their desired outcome. If so, once you have matured it, you can continue to develop the original outcome metaphor and then ask what needs to happen for their developed desired outcome to be achieved.

Example transcript: It becomes a boat

A client, who worked in sales, wanted to be more proactive and outgoing. In this session he had been developing metaphors for two aspects of himself—a soft part which likes to go out quickly, do some work and then hide away, and a prepared part which is like a sword: sharp and precise and focused. He had also mentioned "a very private part".

Client:	... and a compromise takes place between the parts, which is not really anything, but it keeps you busy.
Facilitator:	And when it keeps you busy, what would you like to have happen? (*Checking for desired outcome.*)
Client:	I'd like to have a sales business to be proud of. And it would be nice if the two parts were aligned in some way, if they stopped going backwards and

forwards ... and there was some bringing it together, more of a direction... and it sort of changes when that happens, it's more of a vehicle now. (Client stopped making rocking-back-and-forth gestures and gestured as though to a direct route ahead.) The sword is a weapon and the soft part is something that's hiding. As they come together it becomes a vehicle. (*A change has happened.*)

Facilitator: What kind of vehicle? (*Asking about the change itself.*)

Client: It's got elements of the softness and the sharpness as well. I'm thinking of a boat. The boat has still got that sharpness, and it's got softness, and it can go somewhere. And it can take me with it.

Facilitator: And when it's got elements of the softness and the sharpness, is there anything else about that boat? (*Asking about the change itself.*)

Client: It's a superb image! It's the shape of a fishing boat, with a cabin on the back that the soft bit can go in when it wants to.

Facilitator: And a boat, the shape of a fishing boat, and it's got elements of the softness and the sharpness. And there's a very private part. And when it's the shape of a fishing boat, what happens to the very private part? (*Checking effect of the change on other symbols.*)

Client: It can hide in the cabin as well.

Facilitator: And the shape of a fishing boat. And when it's the shape of a fishing boat, it can go somewhere? (*Checks model.*)

Client: (*Indicates*) In that direction.

Facilitator: And whereabouts in that direction? (*Developing effect of the change over time.*)

Client:	As far as the eye can see.
Facilitator:	And in that direction, as far as the eye can see. And a sales business to be proud of. And when a fishing boat in that direction, as far as the eye can see, what happens to a business to be proud of? (*Checking effect of the change on other symbols.*)
Client:	It becomes much more possible, it feels more possible.
Facilitator:	And as that business to be proud of feels more possible, what happens next? (*Checking effect of the change over time.*)
Client:	I ... Oh! ... I'm starting to feel taller. And it's like, from my boat, I can look customers in the eye more. (*Another change.*)
Facilitator:	And is there anything else about looking them in the eye? (*Asking about the change itself.*)
Client:	Yes ... the softness and hardness of my old 'looks' have come together and now when I look at them, the customer steps willingly into my boat with me.
Facilitator:	And then what happens? (*Checking effect of the change over time.*)
Client:	We go places together, and later he sends his friends and contacts to me ... and the business keeps gathering steam. Amazing!

And the maturing process continued ...

In this example, the italics indicate the aspect of maturing change that the facilitator is focusing on. You can see how the change itself is generally the first aspect the facilitator asks about. After that, questions can be asked about either the effects on other symbols or the effects over time, and very often the two will be intertwined. This transcript is also a good illustration of something else to look out for—when the client surprises themselves. The "Oh!" indicated something unexpected had happened and this often foretells a major shift.

But what if the client encounters a problem during maturing? What if the client's last answer in the example above had been, "Oh … my private part hates having them on my boat. It's like an intrusion."? In this situation, check what the client would like to have happen now (it's very likely that their desired outcome has been updated) and then develop that, incorporating information from the landscape you've already developed where it is relevant. Continue until another change occurs, and then mature that.

When it comes to maturing, the best tip we can give you is this: when you think you've spent enough time maturing the change, its effects over time and its effects on other symbols, spend a little longer. Experienced Clean Language users often spend one-third of their time maturing changes. This phase is an investment in long-lasting change, so don't skimp!

You now have all the building blocks of Clean Language ready for you to help people who wish to make a change in their life. But before you start practising with other people, the next chapter provides two activities structured to help you practise on your own.

Chapter 10
Putting it Together for Yourself

"A journey of a thousand miles begins with one step"
—Lao Tsu

Ready to experience the power of Clean Language for yourself? This chapter brings together what you have learned so far into two opportunities for you to get familiar with the process as a client, before you start to facilitate change with other people. After that, we invite you to start practising on a small scale with others, and offer a transcript of a complete Clean Language session which led to a change.

Self-modelling activities

Clean is mostly used by two people, one asking the questions and the other answering. Working with a facilitator is the most valuable for most people, in most situations. But in many instances the process can also be used on your own, and these activities are written with this in mind—if you prefer, you can adapt them to use with a partner.

Normally, it's the job of the person asking the Clean Language questions to decide which question to ask, and what part of the other person's information to ask about. That's where the artistry of Clean rests.

In these exercises we provide some extra pointers for which questions to use when, and what to ask about. They are based on Penny Tompkins and James Lawley's Framework for Change. Experience suggests this kind of activity assists beginners in getting the best possible results. We'd love to hear how you get on.

In the first activity, you'll be modelling a useful resource by developing a metaphor for it. We've structured it around 'learning at your best'—you could use the same structure to model any skill or ability which you have, and which you value.

The second activity moves on to use Clean in contexts where change is wanted.

Activity 1: When you are learning at your best, you're like what?

For this activity you will need a quiet place, about 30 minutes, a pencil, several sheets of paper and a clock.

The purpose of modelling a useful resource for yourself is that, through the process, you will learn more about how you learn well and what helps or hinders this. With all this information, you will be in a much better position to get into that resourceful state at will, and to prolong it if you wish. In other words, this kind of activity provides a way to have more choice over the mood or state you are in, allowing you to get into an appropriate frame of mind for the situations that you face.

Summary of this activity

Step	Activity	Time
1	Discover your metaphor	5 minutes
2	Develop the attributes of your metaphor	10 minutes
3	Find the sequence and source of your metaphor	7 minutes
4	Discover the conditions necessary for you to access your best learning state	Time as desired
5	Draw or note what you now know	A few minutes

Step 1: Discover your metaphor (5 minutes)

For this activity, start by considering the question, "When you are learning at your best, you are like... what?"

The purpose of this step is to discover a metaphor for yourself when you are learning at your best. You will use this as the starting point for the activity.

For example, a person might be like:

- A butterfly, visiting different flowers and collecting pollen from each.

- An enthusiastic puppy, focusing and delighting in playing ball.

- Someone taking a journey across varied territory.

- A strongly flowing stream, gathering force as it heads towards the sea.

- A light bulb switching on.

- A sponge soaking up new information.

These are just suggestions—your answer will probably be different from any of the above.

Once you have an answer, write it down or, better still, make a quick drawing.

Step 2: Develop the attributes of your metaphor (10 minutes)

Your next task is to spend 10 minutes asking yourself the Developing Questions to find out more about your metaphor. Your objective is to get a detailed 'name and address' for each symbol as well as information about the relationships between the symbols.

Mix up the questions, asking them in any order, and feel free to use the questions more than once.

The Developing Questions are:

— *(And) what kind of X (is that X)?*
— *(And) is there anything else about X?*
— *(And) where is X?* or *(And) whereabouts is X?*
— *(And) that's X like what?*
— *(And) is there a relationship between X and Y?*
— *(And) when X, what happens to Y?*

You may find that, as you uncover more information about your metaphor, you start to experience it. That's a good thing—after all, you are learning at your best right now, aren't you?

Step 3: Find the sequence and source of your metaphor (about 7 minutes)

Next, you are going to spend about 7 minutes asking yourself the Sequence and Source Questions, because in most, if not all, instances, there will be several steps to get you into the state in which you learn at your best. The Sequence and Source Questions will fill in any blanks in the model you've built so far using the Developing Questions.

After considering what you know now, ask yourself:

— *(And) what happens just before X?*
— *(And) then what happens?*

- *(And) what happens next?*
- *(And) where could X come from?*

Again, use the questions in any order that seems appropriate, and ask them more than once. Your objective is to uncover (in metaphor) the sequence of what happens leading up to you learning at your best, through to when you are learning at your best and even just beyond, to when you are no longer learning at your absolute best. This way, you'll be able to spot the clues that let you know where you are in the process of learning at your best in real life, which sets you up for step 4.

Now is also the time to ask yourself the source question. Ask it about any particularly resourceful aspects of your metaphor, and if appropriate, consider asking several source questions in a row, to go further and further back, to reach the original source of the resourceful symbol (e.g. Q: "And where could 'feeling bouncy' come from?" A: "From a spring in my feet." Q: "And where could that spring come from?" A: "From my father's delight in learning." Etc).

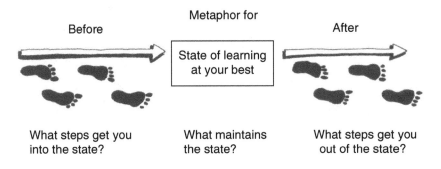

Metaphor for

Before | State of learning at your best | After

What steps get you into the state? | What maintains the state? | What steps get you out of the state?

Step 4: Discover the conditions necessary for you to access your best learning state (as much time as you need)

What needs to happen for you to experience this resource when you need it? For this step, take as much time as you think you need. Repeatedly ask the questions in whatever order seems best to you.

- *(And) what needs to happen for me to experience [my metaphor for learning at my best]?*
- *(And) is there anything else that needs to happen?*

Write down your answer(s) to these questions, listing all the conditions.

Then ask:

- *(And) can [condition] (happen)?*

for each condition that you listed.

For example, if the condition is, "I need to squeeze the sponge out now and then" you would ask, "And can I squeeze the sponge out now and then?"

If you discover that the necessary conditions can happen, that's great. If not, ask:

- *(And) what needs to happen for [condition] (to happen)?*

and keep exploring until you have broken down each condition to components of a size and type that you can achieve.

Step 5: Draw what you now know (a few minutes)

Make a drawing or diagram of what you now know about how you are when you are learning at your best, and include information about the conditions that are necessary to get into this state.

And now you know all this, what difference will it make when you next want to learn at your best?

We have suggested this as a 30-minute activity, but of course modelling activities can be much longer or shorter than 30 minutes. Use these timings to give you an idea of the proportion of time to spend on each step.

Activity 2: A Clean change resolution

For this activity you'll need up to an hour, a quiet place, a pencil and several sheets of paper.

Summary of this activity

Step Activity

1   Build the dream

2   Develop the desired outcome

3   Ask for a metaphor

4   Develop the desired outcome metaphor

4a   Mature any changes

5   Check the sequence and source

6   What needs to happen?

7   Get ready for action

Step 1: Build the dream

Is there something in your life you'd like to change?

Like many New Year's resolutions, your answer may well be about giving something up. You could work with that, but the process of modelling with metaphor works even better when you can say what you'd like *more* of, rather than less of: what you'll be doing with all the time/energy, etc. that you'll have when you don't have the problem any more.

For example, "I'd like to give up smoking," means you'd like *less* of smoking, but it doesn't say what you would like *more* of. So answer the question by stating something you would like more of, e.g. "To taste my food more fully, breathe more easily and have more money to spend on clothes, cars and holidays," or "I'd like hope to triumph over experience." In this context 'triumph of hope' represents something you want more of rather than something you want less of (smoking). We call something you would like more of a 'desired outcome'.

If you have difficulty coming up with what you'd like more of, ask yourself, "When I [have what I want less of] then what happens?" For example, "When I've given up smoking, then what happens?" This question has the effect of focusing attention on the desired outcome.

Another way is to ask yourself, "Could I draw it?" It's not easy to draw *not smoking*, but you could draw a picture of yourself running upstairs two steps at a time with a big smile on your face, showing what you would like instead of smoking.

Once you have a desired outcome to work with, stated in terms of what you want more of, it's time to move to the next step.

Step 2: Develop the desired outcome

Now, use the Clean Language Developing Questions to find out about that desired outcome. Ask questions from this list, in any order:

- *(And) what kind of X (is that X)?*
- *(And) is there anything else about X?*
- *(And) where is X?* or *(And) whereabouts is X?*
- *(And) that's X like what?*
- *(And) is there a relationship between X and Y?*
- *(And) when X, what happens to Y?*

So, we might ask, "And what kind of triumph is that triumph?" or "And is there anything else about hope?" or "And where is that hope?"

Ask yourself these questions, several times, about various words in your desired outcome. In the example, "I'd like hope to triumph over experience," you could ask about 'I', 'like', 'hope', 'triumph' 'over' and 'experience'.

What new ideas come to mind? What new connections seem to form?

Step 3: Ask for a metaphor

Then ask:

– *(And) when all of that, that's like ... what?*

This question invites you to arrive at a metaphor which will encompass some of the key ideas you've come up with. 'Hope triumphing over experience' might be like the end of a *Star Wars* battle scene, featuring an exotic victory parade into a gigantic stadium, or it might be like the joy of placing a perfectly-baked, cinnamon-scented apple cake on the table. For you, it will be something different. In this process there really are no right or wrong answers.

If a metaphor doesn't come to mind after considering the question for a while, imagine that you have achieved your desired outcome. Really imagine living it! Then wonder what this experience is like. What is some other experience that has similar qualities to what you are experiencing? Whatever comes to mind is likely to be a perfect metaphor for your desired outcome (or at least a good first approximation). Do not censor yourself. Trust your intuition to give you an image, sound or feeling that you can use in this activity.

Step 4: Develop the desired outcome metaphor

Now it's time to enjoy developing this metaphor. Think about it. Ask yourself the Developing Questions, which you are already familiar with:

– *(And) what kind of X (is that X)?*
– *(And) is there anything else about X?*
– *(And) where is X? or (And) whereabouts is X?*
– *(And) that's X like what?*
– *(And) is there a relationship between X and Y?*
– *(And) when X, what happens to Y?*

In my example above, I might ask myself, "And what kind of parade is that parade?" or "And where is that parade?" or "And is there anything else about exotic?" or "And when victory parade is exotic, where is exotic?"

Tip: Ask *lots* of 'where' questions. With 'where?' you are attempting to identify where the images/sounds/feelings and thoughts you are having are located *right now*. So I might imagine the victory parade all around me, in front, on both sides and above me. I hear the sounds of cheering people and I feel the 'exotic' as excitement in my tummy.

Feel free to make a few notes. Or just allow your mind to wander, exploring the amazing landscape of thoughts. Occasionally, particularly if you notice your thoughts drifting towards a problem or something you'd like less of, ask yourself:

– *(And) when all of that, what would I <u>like</u> to have happen?*

Stay with the metaphor. There's no requirement to figure out how these 'fantasies' relate to the 'resolution' you first thought of. You may find that your ideas develop and change as you go through this process. For example, my *Star Wars* victory parade might transform from a march to a dance, the music from massed trumpets to acid house. Or the entire metaphor might transform to me sitting quietly by the banks of a river, in tune with nature. Your own imagination holds a much wilder and more far-reaching idea of your potential than any government-sponsored health campaign! These are *your* dreams, *your* hopes, *your* thoughts—allow yourself to go beyond the obvious.

Spend all the time you need to develop your metaphorical desired outcome in exactly the way that is right for you.

Step 4a: Mature any changes

If you notice that something has changed during the process, take some time to mature the change using the Developing Questions and Sequence Questions. For example, if the metaphor has changed from a victory parade to sitting by a river, I could ask myself, "What kind of river?", "Anything else about that river?" and so on. Remember you are searching for a metaphor that most closely represents what you really want.

Step 5: Check the sequence and source

Use the Sequence and Source Questions in any order, as many times as needed, to find out about the order in which things happen within the metaphor and to find the source of useful resources.

- *(And) what happens just before X?*
- *(And) then what happens?*
- *(And) what happens next?*
- *(And) where could X come from?*

Your aim is to find out how the action in the metaphor starts, how it continues and what happens afterwards.

The answers to these questions can help to set this piece of exploration within the context of the rest of your metaphorical world, and check that this is an 'ecological' change for you to make: that is, it fits for the whole of you, that you really want it and that achieving your desired outcome would not have unintended consequences for you, for others in your life or for the planet.

In the example above, I might ask myself, "And what happens just before the victory parade?" or "Where could that exotic victory parade come from?" or "And after the exotic victory parade, what happens next?"

Step 6: What needs to happen?

OK, you've developed a big dream, a metaphor, for the thing you'd like to have happen. Now it's time to check on what conditions are necessary to make this change. Ask yourself:

– *(And) what needs to happen for X?*

(where X is the name of your metaphor or a part of it).

And don't stint on asking, "And is there anything else that needs to happen for X?"

Make a written list of necessary conditions. Ask yourself the question several times, about each key thing that needs to happen, 'drilling down' to a fundamental level. You are looking for the key things which, if they happen, will mean you'll be on your way.

For example, if your first answer to "And what needs to happen for X?" was "A and B", then ask "And what needs to happen for A?" This time your answer is "C", so the next question is "And what needs to happen for C?" and so on. You'll know when to stop when you have the sense that the condition is achievable.

Once you've completed what needs to happen for A, then begin the process again, asking about B and so on.

And when you think you're finally done, ask:

– *(And) is there anything else that needs to happen?*

Your list may be metaphorical ("I need to get an exotic outfit for the victory parade"), or it may refer to real-world actions ("I need to buy nicotine patches"), or it may be a mixture of the two. The exercise will work just as well either way—your other-than-conscious mind knows what it all means.

Tip: It's best not to explore necessary conditions in abstract language; instead, transform them into metaphors, or into actual behaviours, which you will be able to see, hear, feel or do. Abstract language leaves too much 'wiggle room'. When the client says something like "I need to be more easily satisfied" they will have little embodied sense of how that condition will be when it is fulfilled, and therefore they are less likely to action it. However if they get an embodied metaphor for it, they'll be much more likely to do what it takes to be satisfied.

Step 7: Get ready for action

Once you have a complete list of what needs to happen, ask yourself:

– *(And) can [I do what needs to happen?]*

Then go through the conditions (one at a time if necessary) to check each one.

If the answer is 'yes', you are ready to ask yourself another important question:

– *What needs to happen first?*

If you can't (or you won't) do whatever needs to happen, just acknowledge this, give yourself a pat on the back for being so honest, and return to Step 1 to adjust your desired outcome to take your reservations into account.

Ask:

– *(And) when I would like [desired outcome] and I can't or I won't [do the actions that need to happen], what would I like to have happen now?* and start again from the beginning.

What next?

The activities above were written for you to use on yourself. Having done them, now's the time to start practising with other people (face-to-face or on the phone), and you can easily adapt the activities to provide a basic structure for a session.

Activity: Practise, practise, practise

You now have all the fundamental elements of the Clean change process. So find some volunteers to practise with, and get started!

It's best to start small, working with everyday goals and issues, such as staying in a good mood while out shopping with the children or driving in heavy traffic. Move on to tougher challenges as your skill level improves.

If you need anything else to get you started, you could ask yourself Clean Language questions like, "And what needs to happen (for me to get started)?" and, "And can X (happen)?" to work through to what would make your progress easy. Or use Activity 2, above.

After each practice session, spend some time reflecting. What did you do well? What might you do differently next time?

Example transcript: Hot air balloon

Here is an example of a very short Clean session resulting in a change and demonstrating the use of almost all the basic Clean Language questions, facilitated by Wendy. The session was a demonstration during a public telephone seminar.

The facilitator begins by finding out what the client would like (their desired outcome).

Facilitator:	And what would you like to have happen?
Client:	I'd like to let go of my negative self-image and become more true to myself.

Facilitator:	And you'd like to let go of your negative self-image and become more true to yourself. And when become more true to yourself, is there anything else about 'true' like that? (*Asking about attributes of 'true' because it is something the speaker would like more of.*)

Client:	It's about being more assertive.
Facilitator:	More assertive. And when more assertive, what kind of assertive is that assertive? (*Asking about attributes of 'assertive' to develop understanding of the nature of 'true'.*)
Client:	That's about being more accepting of myself.
Facilitator:	More accepting. And when being more accepting of yourself, then what happens? (*Asking about the effects of being 'accepting', to check if it is going to help her achieve what she wants.*)
Client:	Then I feel positive—and <u>free!</u> Which I've wanted for so long.

Now the facilitator thinks that the client has a clear desired outcome ('to become more true to myself and feel positive and free'), she begins to develop it, aiming to get a metaphor for at least part of it.

Facilitator:	You feel positive—and free. And what kind of positive and free is that? (*Asking about attributes of 'positive and free'.*)
Client:	Floating, and effortless and light.
Facilitator:	And floating, and effortless, and light. And whereabouts is that floating, and effortless and light? (*Asking for the address of 'positive and free' by using the attributes 'floating, and effortless and light'.*)
Client:	Sort of all over, and in my upper chest, but also in my thinking, clear in my thinking.

Facilitator:	Sort of all over, and in upper chest, and clear in your thinking. And floating and effortless and light, and that's floating and effortless and light all over, in upper chest and clear in thinking ... like ... what? (*Asking for a metaphor for 'positive and free' by using the name and address information that has been elicited. This maximises the chance that the speaker will be able to access a metaphor.*)
Client:	It's like I'm in a hot air balloon, up in the air, looking down on things. I feel free.

The facilitator sets to work to develop the metaphor 'in a hot air balloon'. At the same time she notes that the word 'free' has come up for a second time, suggesting that it is important, and decides to come back to it a little later.

Facilitator:	And in a hot air balloon, looking down on things and feel free. And is there anything else about being in that hot air balloon? (*Asking about attributes of 'in a hot air balloon'.*)
Client:	I suppose that I can see the bigger picture from here. I've got a different perspective on things.
Facilitator:	And you can see the bigger picture. You've got a different perspective on things. And is there anything else about that perspective as you see the bigger picture?
Client:	I feel calm and relaxed, and I can step back from the situation.
Facilitator:	And calm and relaxed, and can step back from the situation. And in the hot air balloon, looking down on things, and feeling free. And is there a relationship between feeling calm and relaxed and feeling free? (*Returning to 'free' by asking about its relationship to the latest information.*)
Client:	Yes, they go together. They are the same.

The facilitator decides to develop the resource 'calm and relaxed'. She aims to get a metaphor for it, initially by asking Name and Address Questions.

Facilitator:	And calm and relaxed. And whereabouts do you feel calm and relaxed?
Client:	In my forehead and the top of my head.
Facilitator:	And is there anything else about feeling calm and relaxed like that?
Client:	There's brightness.
Facilitator:	What kind of brightness? (*Asking for attributes of 'brightness'.*)
Client:	A warmth.
Facilitator:	And is there anything else about that warmth? (*Asking for attributes of 'warmth'.*)
Client:	I can feel it on my arms as well as on my head.
Facilitator:	And when you feel that warmth on your arms as well as on your head, what kind of warmth is that warmth? (*Continues asking for attributes of 'warmth'.*)
Client:	Pleasant warmth that seems to radiate through the rest of my body. It feels as if it gives me energy.
Facilitator:	And when pleasant warmth that you feel on your arms and on your head, and that radiates through the rest of your body and gives energy, where could that warmth come from?
Client:	Oh! The warmth is the warmth of the burner of the hot air balloon!

There's no need now to ask for a metaphor for 'calm and relaxed'— the client has volunteered one spontaneously. Now the facilitator aims to relate this resource metaphor back to the client's original statement.

| Facilitator: | And warmth is warmth of the burner and it gives you energy and radiates through the rest of your body. And when that warmth radiates through the rest of your body and gives you energy, and in the hot air |

balloon, looking down on things, then what happens to letting go of negative self-image?

Client: I feel like I can leave the negative parts of myself behind … I'm freed from those things now.

The facilitator notices that a change has happened (notice the past tense—"I'm *freed* from those things now") and so moves on to maturing it.

Facilitator: And as I leave the negative parts of myself behind and I'm freed from those things, what kind of I is that I? (*Asking about attributes of 'I'.*)

Client: Fearless, and courageous and really excited.

Facilitator: And fearless, courageous, excited. And when fearless, courageous and excited, and freed from negative parts, then what happens to your self-image? (*Asking about effects on other aspects of the landscape, to mature the change.*)

Client: It has improved already!

Facilitator: And self-image has improved already. And when fearless, courageous and excited, and freed from negative parts and self-image improved, then what happens? (*Asking about effects of change over time to mature the change.*)

Client: I can focus fully now on being true to myself.

The maturing process could have been much more thorough, but time is running out. So the facilitator begins to explore the necessary conditions for the client's desired outcome.

Facilitator: And what needs to happen for you to be true to yourself?

Client: I need to take a risk and be myself. But first I need to accept myself just the way I am. And that means I need to embrace any mistakes I might make and learn from those things.

Facilitator:	Embrace any mistakes and learn. And is there any-thing else that needs to happen for you to accept yourself the way you are? (*Asking about any additional necessary conditions for 'accept myself', which is itself a necessary condition for 'take a risk and be myself'. Note made to come back to 'take a risk' once necessary conditions for 'accepting myself' are explored.*)
Client:	I need to find out more about myself to help me to know who I really am, and then I can be true to myself.
Facilitator:	Find out more about yourself, and embrace mistakes and learn from them, and is there anything else that needs to happen for you to accept yourself just the way you are? (*Checking if there are any additional necessary conditions.*)
Client:	No, I don't think so.

Now the facilitator checks whether the speaker can achieve the necessary conditions for 'accepting myself'.

Facilitator:	And can you find out more about yourself?
Client:	Yes, easily.
Facilitator:	And can you embrace mistakes and learn from them?
Client:	Yes, I can now.
Facilitator:	And then you can accept yourself just the way you are?
Client:	Yes—and then I can take a risk and be myself. (*The client has remembered about 'take a risk' and can do it, so there's no need to ask about it.*)

The facilitator makes a final check for any other necessary conditions for the client to achieve her desired outcome, and draws the session to a close.

Facilitator:	And when you accept yourself just the way you are, and take a risk and be yourself, is there anything else that needs to happen for you to be true to yourself, fearless, courageous and excited?
Client:	No.
Facilitator:	And when all of that, is there anything else that needs to happen for you to feel positive and free?
Client:	No, nothing else.
Facilitator:	And when you can be true to yourself, and fearless, and courageous and excited, up in a hot air balloon looking down on things with bigger picture, negative parts of yourself left behind, with warmth radiating through your body, would that be a good place for us to leave it for now?
Client:	Yes, that's a good place.

A few days later, the client emailed to say:

"I have been amazed at the difference that a few minutes made to me, in that I feel much clearer about what being my 'true self' means to me and I am so excited about the metaphor that emerged, because I had been working on my negative self-image and the fears which were holding me back from being myself.

"I already had the metaphor of the fears being like 'tent pegs'—and now I see that when I am hiding behind my negative self-image—it's like I'm under the tent and when I let go of the fears (tent pegs) which are holding me there, the canvas is released and can form the hot-air balloon in which I'm floating when I'm being my authentic self."

Chapter 11
Directing Attention More Precisely

"Of the good leader, when the task is done, the people will say,
'We did it ourselves'"
—Lao Tsu

By now, you've probably already begun to put Clean thinking into practice. You're beginning to notice metaphors in what people (including you) say. You're listening well, and noticing how differently people see the world. You've started asking Clean Language questions to gather information, to model a resourceful state (e.g. learning at your best) and for personal change.

You've grasped the simple approach:

- Listen attentively
- Remember that your assumptions, opinions and advice are your own
- Ask Clean Language questions to explore a person's words, particularly their metaphors
- Listen to the answers and then ask more Clean Language questions about what they have said.

Is that all there is to it? Well, no. Particularly if you work one-to-one with clients who want to change, there may be some challenges still to come. One of these is at the heart of the Clean change process: the need to accept that when working as a Clean Language facilitator,

The Clean Change Process

Real-life
difficulty

Real-life
changes

Metaphoric landscape changes

you are going to be largely invisible. This is not everyone's cup of tea—it can be satisfying having people say how wonderful your advice and suggestions are.

The payback for being invisible is to be a witness to change happening in the moment. There is always a wonderful logic to how the changes come about. There's the excitement of sharing another person's inner world, uncovering secrets that nobody has ever known before. And there's the opportunity to appreciate the amazing beauty and transformative potential of those metaphoric landscapes. In retrospect, you can spot clues that were there from the start, but there is no shortcut available to you or the client because the changes emerge from going through the process.

Willing to give it a try?

If you want to do a Clean Language 'session', first make sure that you have the client's clearly expressed permission. Sometimes a question like, "Would you be interested in me helping you to explore that now?" or "If you wish, I can ask you some questions to help you find out more about that," can be useful. And if they say no, respect their right to refuse your support, however well-intentioned and however much you just know it would improve their life.

In this chapter, you'll learn some specific approaches used by Clean Language facilitators to keep their work as Clean, and as effective, as possible. In particular, you'll learn how to use syntax and 'zooming in and out' to direct the client's attention precisely.

Full syntax

It's your job as facilitator to actively direct the client's attention. Within Clean Language, a key means for doing this is 'syntax', a subtle way to direct the client's attention to a part or detail of their metaphor landscape. ('Syntax' here means "What goes where, and in what order,"[18] and refers to what you say, and when you say it, when asking a Clean Language question.)

---

[18] Richard Bandler and John Grinder, *Reframing*, 1982.

Making use of syntax is a more sophisticated version of the idea of repeating back a few of the client's exact words, as suggested earlier. One of the hallmarks of Clean Language is the 'full', three-part syntax.

When using full syntax, the facilitator speaks slowly, rhythmically and with curiosity, and follows this pattern:

"And … [client's words or gestures],

and when … [some of client's words or gestures],

[Clean Language Question with some of client's words or gestures]?"

There are three steps:

(1) *Acknowledge* what the client has just said:
    "And … [client's words or gestures],
(2) *Direct their attention* to the part that you intend to ask about:
    and when … [some of client's words or gestures],
(3) *Ask* a Clean Language question:
    [Clean Language Question with some of client's words or gestures]?"

For example:

"And there seems to be a warm light shining through the open door, (1)
and when there's warm light shining, (2)
what kind of light *is that* light?" (3)

Some alternative questions (step 3) would be:

– *is there anything else about that* light? (3)
– *is there anything else about* the warm of that warm light? (3)
– *where is that* light shining? (3)

The first time you do this it may sound or feel strange. As a result, you may be tempted not to bother. But if you persevere, particularly once you and the client feel settled, the full syntax will help take the client deeply into their metaphoric, internal experience. This is the value of using full syntax. And once a client is deeply into their metaphoric experience, that's where the magic happens.

When you repeat the client's words, as you acknowledge, direct their attention and ask your question, it has the added benefit of making their words easier for you, and them, to remember.

Notice that the Clean Language question itself, in step 3 of the syntax, does not start with 'And'. A question will only start with 'and' if the question is used on its own, without the syntax leading up to it.

Activity: Practising full syntax

As you travel, or read a magazine, use sentences or phrases from advertisements to practise your full syntax. It's a great way to learn the syntax effortlessly.

For example, an advertisement reads: "Go to work on an egg."

You say to yourself, "And go to work on an egg, (1)
         and when work on an egg, (2)
            is there anything else about that egg?" (3)

We are indebted to Barbara Houseman for suggesting this activity.

Shortened syntax

We recommend you use all three steps of the syntax until you can do them easily, and then start to vary the amount of syntax you use. Most real-life sessions will contain a mixture of full syntax and a number of shorter versions. So experiment with using only part of the syntax, just steps 1 and 3; just steps 2 and 3, or step 3 (the question) on its own. This last option in particular will sound more like an ordinary conversation. All the variations have their place in working Cleanly.

So if an advertisement reads, "Buy now while stocks last", you could use shortened syntax such as:

"And buy now while stocks last, (1)
(pause) whereabouts are stocks?" (3)

Or perhaps, "And when buy now, (2) what kind of now is that now?" (3)

Or just, "Is there anything else about stocks?" (3)

Once you have the skill to use the full syntax and some of the shorter forms, when is each variation best used?

Use full syntax when:

● The client is exploring new territory and needs time to process
● The client is referring to a sensation inside or around their body
● You want to direct the client's attention with pinpoint accuracy.

Use shortened syntax, or Clean Language questions on their own, when:

● The client's metaphor landscape is changing quickly, 'in front of their very eyes'. You'll want to ask your questions quickly to keep up.
● The context makes a more conversational approach appropriate, for example, when gathering information in a research interview.

'And' not 'so'

Clean Language questions, and the full syntax pattern, are connected using the word 'and'. And this can be addictive!

Some people have a tendency to start their question with 'so', but 'and' gets the best results: 'so' can come across as judgemental, or as if the facilitator is drawing conclusions from what the client said. The repeated use of 'and' lets the client know that the whole inter-action is being conducted from their perspective.

When used before repeating the client's words (step 1), 'and' says, 'And I acknowledge what you have just said, and I am checking that I heard correctly and what I am about to say now is connected to what you have just said.' This near-seamless connection helps the client to stay with their own 'stuff'. And again, the 'and' at the start of step 2 of the sequence also has the function of providing a seamless connection.

Activity: Using random questions and full syntax

Spend 10 or 15 minutes working with a partner to help them to model their metaphor for a resourceful state, such as 'learning at your best' or 'confident just the way you'd like', by combining full syntax with Clean Language questions drawn at random. Experiment with drawing your question at different points in the syntax—before you start, after step 1, or after step 2—and notice what difference this makes.

The syntax offers the facilitator a flexible way to direct the client's attention. Directing the client's attention is *the* tool that the facilitator has for working with the client, so choose with care whether to use the full syntax or a shortened form, and consider carefully which of the client's words to repeat in order to direct their attention to precisely the spot you have chosen.

Backtracking

Once you're comfortable with using the full syntax to ask about the last answer the client gave, you can take your facilitation to the next level and use it to move about freely within all the information the client has given you. One way to do this is an approach called backtracking.

It works like this. In the *acknowledge* section of the full syntax (step 1), lead the client back through the things they've mentioned, until you reach the place or thing in their information to which you want to direct their attention.

So if they have talked about A and B and C, in that order, and you want to ask about A, start by mentioning C, then B and then A, and then ask your question about A. This process provides a series of 'stepping stones' for the client to move their attention. A huge leap straight from C to A might cause them to lose their internal focus and come out of the process, and you will want to avoid this because it is by keeping them processing their 'stuff' that the client self-models and makes changes.

Example transcript: A metaphor for my heart

Client:	I would like to find out more about a metaphor for my heart and how I want my heart to be: big, beating fully and not constrained by so-called 'protection'. (*A*)
Facilitator:	And big, beating fully, not con-strained. And when **that** heart is big, beating fully, is there any-thing else about **that** heart?
Client:	It's redder, and has more oxygenated blood. And it's more variable in size, not just big. And the beating of it is a more obvious feeling, more noticeable. (*B*)
Facilitator:	And it's redder, and has more oxygenated blood. And more variable in size, and a more obvious feel-ing. And when more obvious feeling, where is **that** obvious feeling?
Client:	On the inside, at the centre of my chest. (*C*)

The client has mentioned various attributes of the heart. The failitator now decides to ask about A, so he repeats C, B, and then A, to move the client's attention gradually and avoid startling the client out of their metaphor by a big jump.

> **Facilitator:** And a more obvious feeling at the centre of your chest (*C*), and more variable in size, and redder, more oxygenated blood (B). And big, beating fully, not constrained (*A*). And when 'not constrained', is there anything else about **that** not constrained? ...

Using 'that'

When asking Clean Language questions, facilitators generally don't use 'the' or 'this' when referring to a client's words. If the client says, "It's a translucent sphere, about as big as a basketball," the facilitator asks, "And is there anything else about **that** sphere?" rather than 'this sphere' or 'the sphere'.

The word 'that' makes it clear the sphere belongs with the client, and is not a sphere in the shared space of the facilitator and client. It also makes clear it is that specific sphere, and no other, which is the focus of attention. In the example transcript above, uses of 'that' have been emboldened to provide examples.

Zooming in and out

Once a symbol has been mentioned, Clean Language questions can invite the client to 'zoom in' on it—to find out more about it and bring it more fully into view—and then 'zoom out' again to place it in context.

1. Zooming in

Zooming in makes it easier for the client to differentiate one thing from another and helps them to pay attention to a detail or to notice a resourceful attribute. It is as if the client's attention is being funnelled or focused more and more tightly, like a camera zooming in, until they are attending to a very small part of their landscape.

The most useful questions for zooming in are:

- *(And) what kind of X (is that X)?*
- *(And) where is X?* or *(And) whereabouts is X?*

A common form of zooming in is to start with the metaphor, then zoom into one symbol within the metaphor, and then zoom in again to one attribute of that symbol.

Example transcript of zooming in:
A metaphor for my heart (continued)

Below, notice how the questions zoom in on 'felt connection', which is one attribute of 'easily energetically connected', and the client becomes aware of additional information (underlined).

Facilitator:	And when 'not constrained', is there anything else about not constrained?
Client:	Easily energetically connected with other people.
Facilitator:	And easily energetically connected with other people. And when easily energetically connected, what kind of connected is that easily energetically connected?
Client:	A felt connection, it's not visible.
Facilitator:	And a felt connection, not visible. What kind of felt connection?
Client:	It's a <u>permanent or near-permanent connection.</u>
Facilitator:	And a permanent or near-permanent connection. And whereabouts is the permanent or near-permanent of that connection?
Client:	It's <u>in my heart.</u>
Facilitator:	And in your heart. And whereabouts in your heart is that connection?
Client:	It's <u>in the front and in the back.</u> And there's <u>more than one connection.</u>

2. Zooming out

Zooming out helps the client to 'take a step back' and attend to the 'bigger picture'. Again, using the photograph metaphor, it is as though the facilitator offers them a lens that progressively takes in more and more of the landscape.

The most useful questions for zooming out are:

— *(And) is there anything else about all that?*
— *(And) is there a relationship between X and Y?*
— *(And) when X, what happens to Y?*
— *(And) where could X come from?*

And if you include zooming out in time, then also:

— *(And) then what happens?* or *(And) what happens next?*
— *(And) what happens just before X?*

A common form of zooming out is to start with a symbol, then zoom out to the metaphor and then zoom out again to the landscape.

Example transcript of zooming out:
A metaphor for my heart (continued)

Notice how the questions zoom out, drawing the client's attention to the 'big picture' of the landscape. In this case zooming out enables the client to put 'connection' back into the original context of her desired outcome of finding out more about a metaphor for her heart and how she wants her heart to be. Again, additional information is underlined.

> **Facilitator:** And more than one permanent or near-permanent connection in the front and back of your heart; a felt connection. And when all of that, then what happens to so-called protection?

Client: <u>That protection's gone. My heart is open to others.</u>

Facilitator: And protection's gone, and connections, and heart is open to others, and you'd like your heart to be big, beating fully. And is there anything else about all that?

Client: My heart's not always that big. It varies. But so far, it doesn't seem to go back to as small as it was. When it's big, I'm more aware of <u>how many</u> connections there are. <u>There are a lot of connections</u>, in the front and the back. With that connection, other people will usually say something like, "You're looking amazing!" or they'll spend more time with you, or choose to sit next to you. <u>They also feel that connection</u>.

Facilitator: And a lot of connections, and more aware of connections, and other people feel the connection, and heart beating fully, not constrained. And when all that, is there anything else about that heart being how you want your heart to be and connection to other people?

Client: It's something <u>to do with networks</u>. Not being an end node, but <u>a node with multiple connections</u>, and <u>inward and outward connections</u>. I notice it's not spinning. <u>It may be rotating very slowly</u>. It has <u>a sense of steadiness</u> to it.

Afterwards, the client said she now felt a connection within herself, and wasn't so reliant on other people's opinions.

Ending a Clean Language session

A Clean Language session can be so fascinating that you may want to keep it going. But when you've run out of time or the client asks to stop in order to process what they've discovered, or you seem to have come to a natural place to stop, then find a way to smoothly finish the session.

First, it's a good idea to recap some of the information that has emerged, to help the client remember what they have been paying attention to, and realise how far they have come.

After that, some possible Clean endings are:

- *(And) would this be good place to stop?*
- *(And) would this be good place to leave it for now?*

For example, if the client has mentioned four main things, A, B, C and D, you might end by recapping these four and then checking the client feels that it is a suitable moment to end on, "And when D and B and A and C, would that be a good place to stop?" Notice that it isn't essential to mention A–D in the order they were discussed; rather, repeat them in the logical order of the content.

If the client has not yet got all that they wanted, then as an alternative after recapping you could say:

- *(And) take all the time that you would like to find out more about [desired outcome, or an element of their exploration that they've expressed an interest in knowing more about].*

For example, in the session 'A metaphor for my heart' above, the facilitator might recap, "And networks, and multiple connections, inward and outward, and big heart, and beating fully, and redder, variable in size, and energetically connected, and felt connection noticed by the other person. And take all the time you would like to find out more about how you want your heart to be now."

Assignments

Often the information that emerges in a session is a new discovery for the client, and it will continue to develop during the hours and days after the session. Giving them tasks can stimulate this natural process, and encourage them to continue self-modelling after the session.

Some common kinds of tasks include:

- Making a drawing or sketch of the metaphors that emerged in the session. This is so they capture what they have discovered and what may subsequently emerge. If there are to be several sessions, ask the client to update their drawing before their next session. It is often useful to start a subsequent session with the client's description of their updated drawing(s).
- Taking some time to think about what has emerged and what they would like to have happen as a result.
- Looking up the meanings and derivation of unique or significant words, labels or symbols that appeared in the session. A comprehensive dictionary is useful to get full value from this, or they could use online resources. The idea isn't for the client to take on board any or all meanings of the words they research, but rather for them to become aware of what resonates with their metaphor landscape. For example, when Wendy was working as a client with having 'either X or Y' she looked up 'either' and realised it can be used to mean 'both' (as in, 'there was a window at either end of the room'). The idea of 'both' gave her the chance to reconsider the whole way she was thinking of her situation.
- Trying out new behaviours which may have come up during the session. This can help to ground the client's learnings in their daily life.

To illustrate, at the end of the session 'A metaphor for my heart', the facilitator set her client the following tasks:

- Look up 'heart' and pay attention to the origin of the word (its etymology).
- Find out about the mechanics of how hearts work.
- Draw what you now know.

Activity: Investigating significant symbols

Consider the symbols and words you have used in the activities so far. Which ones seem to you to have the most significance? Using a dictionary containing the derivation of words (etymology) and/or books of symbols, look up the ones you have identified as the most significant. Does anything you read lead to further insights for you?

* * *

Some of the books we have found useful for this are:

Ayto, John, *Bloomsbury Dictionary of Word Origins*, Bloomsbury, 1990

Ayto, John (ed), *Brewer's Dictionary of Phrase and Fable*, Weidenfeld and Nicolson, 2002

Barnhart, Robert (ed), *Chambers Dictionary of Etymology*, Chambers, 1988

The Chambers Dictionary, 10th edn, Chambers, 2003

Cooper, J. C. (ed), *An Illustrated Encyclopaedia of Traditional Symbols*, Thames and Hudson, 1979

Shepherd, Rowena and Rupert, *1000 Symbols: What Shapes Mean in Art and Myth*, Thames and Hudson, 2002

Chapter 12
Beyond Words and Into Space

*"It requires a very unusual mind to undertake the analysis
of the obvious"*
—Alfred N. Whitehead

Human beings have bodies and live in space. Everyone knows that
we are not disembodied minds, and the way we think is based in
our physical, embodied experience. Obvious as this seems, it has
major implications.

Whenever we see, hear or feel something, we see, hear or feel it
somewhere in space. And the metaphors we use are grounded in the
reality of being a person living in a body, influenced by gravity. So,
in Clean Language facilitation, space is accorded a special significance. The facilitator keeps their space to themselves and focuses
their attention on the client's space. You would never dream of
moving someone's physical belongings around in their office or
home—and in a Clean Language session we extend the same
respect to the location of the client's symbols in their imaginative
space.

Beginning a Clean Language session

A Clean Language session is carried out from the client's perspective. Although the client may not be consciously aware of it, where
they are in the room and in relation to the facilitator can make a big
difference to how readily they can attend to their metaphor landscape. So at the start of a session, it's usual to ask the client to
choose where they would like to be in the room and where they
would like you to be:

– *And where would you like to be?*
– *And where would you like me to be?*

The order is important, first the client positions themselves and then they position the facilitator.

Once you are both seated, the usual opening question is:

– *And what would you like to have happen?*

Before a meeting or session, set up the room so the client has a real choice of where to sit or stand. Remove your belongings, stand up and move away from 'your' chair before you ask. This sends an important message—this session is about them, not you. Being able to place themselves and you in an optimal position can enhance their ability to think, learn and grow.

As the client selects where to sit, they may be unaware of the reasons behind their choice. But, like their words and the non-verbal elements of their communication, this choice can prove to be metaphoric, or 'point' to metaphoric information. David Grove said that in choosing where to sit, and where to place the facilitator, the client is aligning the metaphor landscape with the physical space. So it's not unusual for furniture and fittings in a room, innocuous at the start of a session, to start to play a part in the client's metaphoric landscape and they will often turn out to be in 'just the right place'.

Activity: Where is your best place to be a client?

Where, in your home or office, is the best place for you to be a client in a Clean Language session?

Start by deciding on a desired outcome for yourself to work with and writing it on a piece of paper. Take it with you as you try different spaces in different rooms. If location seems to make no difference to you, try going to extremes: the very corner of the attic, under the table, the bathroom etc. You could even try sitting in 'someone else's chair'. Notice what happens.

Ideally, do this with a friend, imagining them as your facilitator as you place them in relation to you in the various places you try. Spend a minute or two in each place and notice how you react to being there. What in the environment is having the most effect on you?

* * *

Compare and contrast your experience with that of your friend.

❖ A coaching client was working on a major life transition and her metaphor was of going through a door to a new world. As the metaphor developed, the door of the physical room began to represent her metaphorical, imaginary door … which meant she could choose to stand up, open it, and experiment with going through it, there and then. Surprising new insights resulted. She said, "It was very exciting! I never thought that I could actually go through the door—then suddenly, I was on the other side of it, where things looked completely different. I suppose it's really only an ordinary door, but it felt very dramatic. And having gone through it during the session meant that I had a taste of what the change would be like in real life, which made me want it even more."

Language highlights how central (!) space is to us. Steven Pinker, in *How the Mind Works*, says that "location in space is one of the two fundamental metaphors in language" (the other is force). He writes, "A handful of concepts about places, paths, motions … underlie the literal or figurative meanings of tens of thousands of words and constructions, not only in English but in every other language that has been studied."[19] He suggests that space as a metaphor is so central to our thinking that it is like the medium of thought.

Spatial metaphors in language

Some examples of language in which space is used as a metaphor are:

- Going forward
- A turning point
- Put it to one side
- Go off track in a meeting
- Beside myself
- On the emotional level
- In the depths of depression
- Jump ahead
- Career path.

Some of the most common words in English—the prepositions (in, on, at, near, by, for, under, before, after, etc.)—refer to spatial relationships, real or (mostly) metaphorical. And it's difficult to think about time without using a spatial metaphor: time passes, flies, drags, *on* Thursday, *in* summer, and so on.

Even a client who talks very abstractly will be using spatial metaphors. Listen out for them—they can be a great way to model the client's metaphoric landscape. For example, if someone says: "The senior manager is always *in* the way when we want to be innovative," it's a spatial metaphor. You could ask "And is there anything else about *in*, when she is always *in* the way?" or "Whereabouts is 'the way'?"

To improve your spatial metaphor spotting skills, look out for them in whatever you read. Almost any piece of writing will be full of them. Look at this well-known paragraph by Marianne Williamson in *A Return to Love*:

---

[19] Steven Pinker, *How The Mind Works*, 1997, pp. 354–357.

"We ask ourselves, who am I to be brilliant, gorgeous, talented, fabulous? Actually, who are you not to be? You are a child of God. Your playing small doesn't serve the world. There's nothing enlightened about shrinking so that other people won't feel insecure around you. We are all meant to shine, as children do. We were born to make manifest the glory of God that is within us. It's not just in some of us; it's in everyone. And as we let our own light shine, we subconsciously give other people permission to do the same. As we're liberated from our own fear, our presence automatically liberates others."

The spatial metaphors we noticed are italicised below:

"We ask ourselves, who am I to be brilliant, gorgeous, talented, fabulous? Actually, who are you not to be? You are a child of God. Your playing *small* doesn't serve *the world*. There's nothing enlightened about *shrinking* so that other people won't feel insecure *around* you. We are all meant to shine, as children do. We were born to make manifest the glory of God that is *within* us. It's not just *in* some of us; it's *in* everyone. And as we let our own light shine, we subconsciously give other people permission to do the same. As we're *liberated from* our own fear, our *presence* automatically *liberates* others."

We don't claim that our assessment is definitive. We may have missed some, and in some cases you may not agree that a word is a spatial metaphor. But we think you'll agree that plenty of spatial metaphors have been used.

Activity: Musical space

Many titles of popular songs include spatial metaphors. Working alone or with a friend, take a trip down memory lane and see how many you can list. Tip: '*in* love' is a spatial metaphor.

Here are a few from Elvis to get you started:

- *In* The Ghetto
- *Little* Sister
- Puppet *On* A String
- *Return* To Sender
- Santa *Bring* My Baby *Back To* Me.

We are indebted to Paul Tosey for this idea.

Space in a Clean Language session

As we mentioned when introducing the question

– *And where/whereabouts is X?*

the things that a client mentions will usually exist 'somewhere': that is, they will have a spatial location within their imagination or, as cognitive scientists call it, their 'mental space'.

Over the course of a Clean Language session, a client will often construct an entire landscape of metaphoric symbols, and the relationships between them, using the space in their bodies. They may also populate the space around their bodies with symbols, locating symbols in front of them, behind them, above them, below them and/or alongside, all at various distances.

When symbols have clear locations in space, what we have called 'addresses', the facilitator's life is easy. That's one of the reasons that it is good practice to ask lots of location questions. It's also good practice to imagine the client's symbols in and around them, placing them exactly in the places the client has indicated. Then, it's much easier for both facilitator and client to understand the spatial relationships between the symbols, to notice any startling gaps and to shift attention around the landscape. This embodied experience of their metaphoric landscape may be new for the client, and can have a significant emotional impact. For many clients it's like looking in a mirror for the first time.

❖ A coaching client, exploring relationships between aspects of his work, was asked lots of location questions. He found he could arrange the aspects in a simple network, shaped like a triangle with himself at the inside centre. As he continued to explore, he chose to adjust some of the distances between the aspects and himself until he had created the precise balance he wanted—and which he was later able to create in his real, working life.

❖ A 14-year-old girl was in trouble at school after kicking a classmate in the head. After some discussion about how extreme the classmate's provocation had been, she told her counsellor, "It was like holding chocolate under a dog's nose—the dog can't resist gobbling it down." The girl felt she had no choice in the situation: the ongoing provocation was, for her, like chocolate held out to a dog, and so she kicked.

With Clean questioning, she explored a 10-step scale of 'closeness of chocolate to dog' which ranged from chocolate not in the same room as the dog, through to chocolate in the same room but well out of reach, all the way to chocolate right under the dog's nose. Having developed this spatial metaphor for her experience, she said, "Now let's do the same thing with people."

With further questioning, she established a 10-step scale for her metaphorical 'closeness to being provoked into kicking'. She marked out this scale spatially, using the width of the room and taking a big step each time she started to consider the next 'step' on her scale. The scale ranged from her being completely relaxed and happy, to getting hot all over, then her legs and arms getting tight, to a feeling of being about to burst, to having no control over her actions at all.

With this established, she was facilitated to explore her emotional response to each of the steps on the scale. Particular attention was paid to the threshold beyond which it was probable that she would kick. This meant she could monitor her state throughout the school day and take action to change her state if she found herself heading for that threshold.

Eye contact

In many coaching methodologies, rapport with the client—often indicated by lots of eye contact—is seen as central. In Clean Language, however, our aim is to be in rapport with the client's *information*. So a Clean Language facilitator will aim to 'make eye contact' with the symbols by looking at them and/or gently gesturing to where they are in the client's space, as though they were real. This acknowledges and honours the symbols, breathing life into them, and helps the client to keep thinking, keep exploring and keep finding new information. Unless you look and gesture to where their symbols are located, you will be forcing the client to focus attention on 'translating' your gesture, or your look, back into what makes sense to them, and this will take their attention away from full involvement in exploring their metaphoric landscape.

Think of a time when you asked someone for directions. As they told you "First left, second right ..." etc. you probably stopped making eye contact with them, to enable you to make your own internal map of the route. We take in so much information from eye contact that it can limit how much processing power we have available for other tasks. As a Clean facilitator, you will help your clients to focus fully on their internal experience if you reduce eye contact with them and put it on their symbols instead.

In this way, the client can develop a close relationship with their metaphoric landscape, rather than a close relationship with you as facilitator. The more they do this, the more the location and nature of the symbols will pose their own questions to the client. You know the process is working when they start to wonder about how their landscape is organised and how it might change—without you even asking a question.

Gestures and other non-verbals

You may have been taught that in 'body language' a particular gesture *means* a particular thing, such as 'arms folded' *means* 'don't talk to me'. In fact, people's gestures and other non-verbal signals can be as brilliantly unique as their words. And Clean Language is a great way to explore them.

This can be particularly useful because people are usually unaware, or only half aware, of their non-verbals, yet these may contain valuable information. Non-verbals can be closely related to symbols in the client's landscape, and especially to the *location* of those symbols.

In Clean Language, any non-verbal—sound, gesture or movement —can be treated as though it were a word, e.g. "And is there anything else about [make the same sound, gesture or movement as the client]?"

Examples of non-verbals might include:

Sounds	**Body**
Clearing the throat	Gestures
Coughs	Movements
Grunts	Twitches
Sighs	Body positions
Mmm, um	Facial expressions
Humming	Breathing changes
Laughter	Twirling hair
Yawning	Smoothing clothes
Exclamations	Clasping hands
	Rubbing
	Acting out the metaphor

Activity: Noticing non-verbals

Record a TV chat show. When you watch it, ignore what is being said (try turning down the sound).

Instead, practise noticing the non-verbals.

Start by just attending to gestures—use the slow motion facility if necessary.

Then move on to spotting gestures that are repeated. Do you notice any patterns in a person's gestures, e.g. lots of choppy or rounded ones? Try fast-forwarding to see repeating patterns over time.

When noticing gestures is no longer challenging, you can turn your attention to non-verbal sounds. Listen out for sounds that are repeated.

Then consider whether there is a relationship between the sounds and any of the gestures.

Finally move on to listening to what the person is saying while still tracking the non-verbals, and start to guess which non-verbals it might be worth asking Clean Language questions about.

* * *

Is there a difference between noticing gestures and noticing non-verbal sounds? Is one easier for you? If so, you can put particular attention on the other in future!

Some non-verbal signals may be more relevant to the material than others. Noticing any recurrence of a non-verbal in relation to the client's words or reactions can help you decide whether to draw your client's attention towards it. Pay particular attention to anything unusual and repeated.

Don't use your own words to name a sound or body communication. Instead of saying, "And is there anything else about that spiralling down gesture?" where 'spiralling down gesture' are your words, rather replicate the gesture, 'sketch it out' with your body or hand, point to or look (eye-point) to the place where the client made the gesture or movement. If you point to the position of a gesture in space, point 'gently' rather than 'stabbing' at its location. Also make sure you look or gesture towards the relevant place in the *client's* space (*not* the equivalent space inside or around you) when referring to something that they did with their body.

For example, if the client refers to something gesturing down on their left, and you are sitting opposite them, don't make a gesture down to the side of you. Instead make a gesture which points to the same place they did, to a space down to their left.

Note: Beware of 'conducting' while facilitating, waving your hands or arms in time to your speech. This is something that many people do when learning to facilitate. Some clients won't notice it but it will distract others. Those gestures are yours, not the client's. Keep it Clean!

❖ In a demonstration session during a long answer, David Grove noticed the client tap his wristwatch, twice. "Is there anything else about that <tap tap>?" he asked. The client later said that moment was the turning point for the session. Although he had been completely unaware he was making the gesture until he was asked about it, each tap turned out to have special significance for him.

From a map into space

If you begin a session with a client's drawing or diagram (a 'map' in Clean jargon), it's helpful to both you and the client to get things placed in 'real' space. When you can refer to the client's landscape by gesturing to their symbols around them, in three-dimensional space instead of on their map, it is more likely that the client will start to experience their landscape as being real, rather than talk *about* it. As this happens, there is a much greater likelihood that the client's three-dimensional experience in the session will translate into changes in their life.

Once the client has described their map, ask them a location question about one of the symbols on the map, while indicating the space around them by a sweeping gesture or glance. Do the same with other symbols on the map. Once the client has told you where each of their symbols is located, stop looking at the map, and start looking at the locations of symbols in space whenever you mention them. This will encourage the client to continue the work in the three-dimensional environment in and around them.

Transforming a feeling into a metaphor

As with other symbols, any emotional or physical feeling is likely to exist 'somewhere' in space—most often inside, on or around the client's body. David Grove (and/or his then wife, Cei Davies) devised a Clean three-step routine for modelling feelings, and developing metaphors for them.

Step 1: Where is the feeling?

When the client mentions a feeling, establish its location by asking:

- *(And) where is X (where X is the feeling word)?*
- *(And) whereabouts is X?*

Ask several 'where' and 'whereabouts' questions one after another, so that the client is paying attention to the precise location of their feeling or sensation.

Step 2: What qualities does the feeling have?

Establish the attributes of the feeling by asking:

- *(And) when X is [location], what kind of X (is that X)?*
- *(And) when X is [location], is there anything else about that X?*

If the client is having difficulty describing the feeling then you could also ask:

- *(And) does X have a size or a shape?*

This is one of the 'specialised' Clean Language questions (see Chapter 13) and it helps clients convert abstract concepts into embodied metaphors.

Step 3: Develop a metaphor for the feeling

The client may have given you a metaphor by now, but if not, then ask the metaphor question to invite one:

- *(And) that's X like what?*

where X is the *qualities of the feeling*, rather than the *name* of the feeling. Using the information from the client's answers to your questions is very important here. For example, if the client says their calmness is a warm and moving feeling, ask "That's warm and moving like what?" and *not* "That's calmness like what?"

This process directs a client's attention towards a particular feeling and then keeps their attention on it. They may well experience the feeling more intensely in the process of developing the metaphor, as well as finding that they can more easily access the feeling after the session. So it's most useful and enjoyable to use this process to develop metaphors for feelings the person likes or wants more of.

❖ Judy loves to feel busy, and wanted to find out more about how she does so many things at once. As the facilitator asked lots of 'where?' questions about the busy feeling, Judy discovered that it filled her whole body, but was particularly noticeable in her fingers and toes. It was a "wiggly, lively and energetic" feeling with lots of movement—Judy wiggled from side to side and waved her hands as she described it—and it had a stylish hint of showmanship.

"And that's wiggly, lively and energetic like ... what?" the facilitator asked. After a few minutes' thought Judy replied, "It's like a clockwork octopus on a unicycle!" This metaphor has since been valuable to her in many ways—not least when she realises that her clockwork has run down and it's time to get off the unicycle and rest until the spring is rewound. It has also been valuable to Wendy, who no longer gets concerned by Judy having a huge pile of work on her desk, provided the clockwork appears to be wound up.

Example transcript: Calmness

Client:	... and calmness.
Facilitator:	And when calmness, where is that calmness?
Client:	Here. (*Pats stomach.*)
Facilitator:	Whereabouts here? (*Gesturing to client's stomach.*)
Client:	It starts in my belly, and kind of washes up towards my chest area.
Facilitator:	And in your belly, and washes up towards your chest area. And whereabouts in your belly?
Client:	Like in the centre of my abdomen, so below my diaphragm ..., here. (*Gestures.*)
Facilitator:	And in the centre of your abdomen, below your diaphragm, inside, and washes up towards your chest area. And when it starts in your belly, and washes up towards the chest area, does it have a size or a shape?

Client:	It's quite big. Not a fixed shape, it's moving. It's warm.
Facilitator:	And calmness, quite big, not a fixed shape, starts in your belly, and washes up towards the chest area. And that's ... warm and moving and washes up ... like ... what?
Client:	It's calmness that's like a warm sort of fluid, or an energy, kind of like a radiance. So it feels that it's calmness like a warm radiance.
Facilitator:	Like a warm radiance. And is there anything else about that radiance?
Client:	It feels that it has healing properties ...

The 'feeling to metaphor' routine is so useful because it can be applied whenever a client says, "I feel ..." and the chances are that is going to happen somewhere in a session. Of course, it is up to you as facilitator to choose the most appropriate feelings to convert into metaphor, depending on the client's desired outcome.

Activity: Transforming a feeling to a metaphor

Pick a time when you are experiencing a feeling that you like (maybe it is happening right now) and ask yourself the questions in the three steps above, to get a sense of how this process works and to give you a metaphorical model for that feeling.

Then get the agreement of several friends or colleagues to practise using the feeling to metaphor routine, so that you learn to adjust it to fit the particular responses of each person.

* * *

When you have done this activity several times, consider:

● Did asking several location questions help the client to get more specific about where they were experiencing their feeling?
● How often did the client give you a metaphor, before you asked for one? If it happened, did you notice quickly that they had given you a metaphor?

Enacting the metaphor

This approach can be thought of as the client 'acting' their metaphor. It provides a way to help the client attend to more of the whole of their landscape, and as they do so, they can start to notice what was not found in the individual parts. Sometimes this awareness is all that is needed for change to happen.

Activity: Enacting your metaphor

This activity needs a fairly well-developed current metaphor land-scape to experiment with. Choose three or four symbols and, in turn, visit the places in which they are located. At each location, 'be' the symbol, and make a note of what it knows, what it is noticing, how it is relating to other symbols and what it would like to have happen.

To help a client enact their metaphor, start by using Clean Language to develop a metaphor landscape and then invite them to move to the location of their various symbols. They then move around their metaphor landscape, embodying the symbols, speaking from each location and noticing their changing sense of how the landscape works.

You could start with one of these approaches:

- Ask, "And would you be interested in going there?" and point to the location of one of the symbols.
- If a client shows any inclination to stand up or move within their landscape, encourage this, using as few words as possible.

Then use Clean Language questions, directing the client's attention to what they know from where they have moved to.

❖ Some years ago, Wendy was working on a desired outcome 'to live life with a light touch'. In her metaphor landscape there was a little girl, a mother, sunshine and space surrounding them.

Wendy enacted her metaphor landscape outdoors in the coun-tryside on a summer's day, stepping into being the little girl first, and then the mother.

From being the little girl she got a strong sense of that little girl's wish to have fun, and to have time to notice and appreciate beauty. Wendy did both: she picked and ate cherries from a near-by tree before spitting the pips as far as she could, she ran and skipped and laughed. And she spent time gazing at the beauty of the surrounding corn fields with their swaying, golden crop against the blue sky.

Moving to the mother's location, Wendy 'became' the mother and knew that she needed space and time to breathe. Wendy (being mother) moved to a place where she could get the feel of having the space of the fields around her, and she aligned herself in relation to the paths through the corn to get an experience of having a path to walk along. The mother wanted to move at a speed that was comfortable and Wendy experienced that by an unhurried walk around the landscape, appreciating the birds singing and the wind on her face as well as the warmth of the sun.

A few weeks afterwards, Wendy bought a pair of shoes unlike any others she owned: very high heels, pointy toes, deep pink satin, with shiny 'diamonds' on them. To Wendy it seemed as if from the mother's point of view they were 'ridiculous', but the little girl was delighted with them. The 'mother' could not fail to notice her daughter's joy, and this led to a change in how much of a free rein the little girl should be given—making it easier for Wendy to live life with a light touch.

Clean Space and Emergent Knowledge

In the last years of his life, David Grove's work focused on space. The details of the resulting processes, such as Clean Space and Emergent Knowledge, are beyond the scope of this book. They involve moving the client repeatedly from one physical space to another and another, developing a network which results in the emergence of new information. The client models themself, learning from the embodied experience of the process.

These exciting ways of working open up a wealth of additional Clean approaches for facilitating individuals and groups, some of which can be used alongside Clean Language.

More information about the work is available at http://www.clean language.co.uk or on relevant Clean Change Company courses.

Chapter 13
Frequently Asked Questions

"What people really need is a good listening to"
—Mary Lou Casey

Q: **My client talks a lot. How do I decide which of their words to ask my question about?**

A: Most importantly, has the client got a clear desired outcome? If not, helping them to become clear about what they want is your first priority. If they have got one, then:

- Ask your questions about their desired outcome, resources and other positive aspects of their experience
- Ask your questions about metaphors and metaphoric words rather than any story or explanation they may be giving
- Keep modelling. Which question will help you and your client to complete the picture of what's going on? Are there any notable gaps, such as a missing stage in a sequence?

Put your focus on modelling a specific thing—a particular part of the desired outcome landscape or a key sequence—rather than aiming to skate lightly over the entire situation. Directing attention to the specifics of a metaphor landscape will often provide valuable new information for the client. This may not be a transformation of the whole landscape, but you never know what effects even a small change will have in the long run.

The client's attention may well be caught by interesting side-tracks. If so, it is your responsibility to keep bringing their attention back to modelling their desired outcome metaphor. Don't be easily 'brushed aside'—if necessary ask questions repeatedly to ensure any gaps are filled in (while accepting that if your client says they don't know, they probably don't know, yet). This is particularly relevant when modelling a sequence, so make sure the order logically hangs together, with each step following from the previous one. If it doesn't make sense to you, there may be something missing.

If all else fails, ask about the last thing the client said, since this is the most up-to-date information from their system.

If they can't come up with a desired outcome, you could help them to model a resourceful aspect of their current experience.

Q: Is there anything I can do to maximise the likelihood of the client making their desired change in the real world?

A: Once you're thoroughly familiar with following the guidelines above, there's another level of sophistication. How can you direct the client's attention such that they have a real, live, embodied experience of what is being modelled, right here and now? The more they can have a physical experience of the change, the more their system will learn what needs to happen for them to make the change they want.

Also, if the client would like to feel differently about something, they may benefit from the 'feeling to metaphor' routine (see Chapter 12). In other words, use metaphor to help them to feel their desired feeling very vividly during the session. Having a metaphor for this experience may well make it easier to access in other contexts. If they keep a picture of their metaphor on display in the relevant contexts, it can enhance this process.

While facilitating, you may also notice examples of the client 'doing their outcome'. For example, a client may say, "I want to be more assertive" and behave in a very assertive way during part of the session. It can be helpful to draw the client's attention to the new behaviour by asking Clean Language questions about it in relation to their desired outcome. But beware—your impression of their behaviour is still only your impression! Take care to stay Clean by asking, "And you want to be more assertive. And is there a relationship between you being assertive and saying 'No, I don't want to focus on where assertiveness comes from, I want you to help me work out how to be more assertive with authority figures'?" If there is a relationship, and the client realises they are being assertive with an authority figure, they may realise they are 'doing' their desired outcome. This is more than just a rehearsal; they will be able to notice new information about their experience while they are actually having it. This kind of experience (called 'going live' in Clean Language jargon) significantly increases the chance of clients getting results in the original context.

Q: How do I keep my attention focused? All the client's information seems so interesting!

A: When facilitating, one way of keeping your attention focused is to use the Traffic Light Model devised by Caitlin Walker of Training Attention.[20]

Draw four concentric circles on a sheet of paper. In the centre, write the piece of the client's information on which they want to focus (their desired outcome or their metaphor for their desired outcome). As you take notes of the client's information, the spaces, labelled Green, Amber and Red, are used to indicate how far away you have directed their attention from their central focus.

If you ask about something in the centre circle, the answer belongs in the Green area. If you ask about something in the Green area, the answer goes in Amber. If you ask about something in Amber, the answer goes in the Red area. Once you are in the Red, it's time to backtrack and direct your next question to something closer to the focus—the words in the Green or Amber areas or in the centre circle.

Caitlin Walker's Traffic Light Model

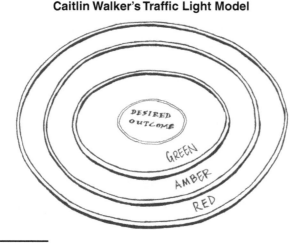

---

[20] Please reference http://www.trainingattention.co.uk when using this model.

For example:

Desired Outcome: "I want to go for a walk." (Centre circle)
Question: "And what kind of walk?"
Answer: "A long one." (Green area)
Question: "And is there anything else about long?"
Answer: "A few miles in the sunshine." (Amber area)
Question: "And what kind of sunshine?"
Answer: "Warm and pleasant." (Red area)

Using this model the next question should not be about "warm and pleasant" but should be about either:

"A few miles in the sunshine." (Amber area)
"A long one." (Green area) or
"I want to go for a walk." (Centre circle).

For example, the next question could be "And warm and pleasant sunshine and you want to go for a long walk. And when want a walk, whereabouts is that want?" Their answer to this question would go in the Green area.

Notice that in this example, the client could be talking about a real walk or a metaphorical one.

Some facilitators use paper with pre-drawn circles to take their notes during a session. This way they are always aware of where their questions are in relation to the client's current desired outcome. If, as frequently happens, the client updates their outcome during a session, it's time to begin a new sheet with the new desired outcome in the centre circle.

You may also choose to use this model to explore a particular symbol, in which case the symbol goes in the centre circle.

Activity: Using the traffic light model

To get a sense of using this method of keeping yourself outcome-focused, draw traffic light rings on a sheet of paper and facilitate your partner, writing each answer in the appropriate ring.

* * *

> What was the effect of this on you as facilitator? Did it change the focus of your attention? Were there times when you decided to start a new set of circles with a resource in the centre, rather than the desired outcome?

Q: What else should I look out for when modelling?

A: Many clients find that one of the most valuable aspects of Clean Language facilitation is becoming aware of the repeating patterns in their own landscape, so that they can work with them rather than against them. A good facilitator spots these patterns and can direct attention to them, Cleanly.

You can only be sure something is a pattern when it has happened at least three times. So expect to have seen/heard at least three instances before hypothesising that it might be a pattern for that client.

Some examples of patterns in symbols and landscapes:

- Shapes (e.g. lots of round symbols).
- Sizes (e.g. client drawing themselves proportionally small relative to other symbols in their drawings).
- Colours (e.g. a number of symbols being the same colour even though they are very different things). This is especially true when the symbols represent different time periods, such as the past and the future.
- Numbers (e.g. a pattern of having three of each of a number of symbols: e.g. three bridges, three butterflies, three angry wasps).
- Spacing between symbols (e.g. symbols all crammed together).
- Location of symbols (e.g. various fearful feelings in the same place, say the stomach).
- Relationships between the symbols (e.g. a number of symbols, each being overwhelmed by other symbols).
- A number of symbols or attributes having the same source (e.g. coming from parents) or the same kind of source.
- A number of symbols having the same function or intention (e.g. all wanting to help).

You may also notice patterns in a person's behaviour:

- Gestures (e.g. various gestures to left temple)
- Habits (e.g. always/never punctual)
- A word used repeatedly (e.g. It's likely you've spotted the pattern by now—Wendy uses the word 'likely' frequently).

Remember, we all have patterns. Your job as facilitator is to pick out the ones that support or hinder a person achieving their desired outcome.

As you develop your Clean facilitation skills, it's important to become aware of your own patterns, since they will inevitably influence your facilitation. There are a couple of reasons this is important.

"Once upon a time there was a therapist who believed that having fish in your dreams was the root of all psychological problems. People would come to him and start telling him about their problems and he'd interrupt and ask …

T: Excuse me, but you didn't happen to have a dream last night, did you?

C: I don't know … I guess maybe I did.

T: You didn't dream about fish, did you?

C: Ah … no … no.

T: What was your dream about?

C: Well, I was walking down the street.

T: Were there any puddles along the gutter?

C: Well I don't know.

T: Could there have been?

C: I suppose there could have been water in the gutter or something.

T: Could there have been any fish in those puddles?

C: No … No.

T: Was there a restaurant on the street in the dream?

C: No.

T: But there could have been. You were walking down the street weren't you?

C: Well I guess there could have been a restaurant.

T: Was the restaurant serving fish?

C: Well, I guess a restaurant could be.

T: Ah ha! I knew it. Fish in the dreams."[21]

If any particular symbol is significant for you—a fish in a dream, for example—you will tend to notice it and to assume it's important for others, when in fact that symbol may be totally irrelevant for them. By knowing your own patterns, you can begin to compensate for these mistaken assumptions, and stay as Clean as possible.

Activity: Pattern-spotting in metaphor maps

Collect all your metaphor maps and spread them out. Now look for patterns. You won't necessarily find patterns that apply across every one, but you will probably be able to spot some that appear in several. You could reflect on the significance of this for you and what you'd like to have happen now that you have noticed them.

You are also likely to have patterns in the questions you ask, with one or two favourite Clean Language questions and one or two you seldom ask. Again, knowing about this will give you the option of extending your range of questions, giving you greater flexibility.

Q: What's the best way of remembering what your client has said?

A: There are as many strategies for this as there are modellers. Some strategies will be more successful than others, and some will be more appropriate, depending on the circumstances. For example, you might remember

---

[21] From Robert Dilts, Tim Hallbom and Suzi Smith, *Beliefs*, 1990.

differently when working on the phone than when working face-to-face. Below is a selection of ideas that we have found helpful.

Remembering without external aids:

- Listen exquisitely. This involves being curious, engaging your brain, having your attention on the client and silencing your internal dialogue.
- Review repeatedly. Say and picture the client's words and symbols to yourself while they are processing.
- Repeating something out loud is helpful: use the full syntax and recap periodically. You'll benefit from this side effect and soon find your memory improving.
- Focus on the middles. It is easier to remember what comes first and last, so go over the middle bits of what a client says more often.
- The more deeply you process the information, the easier it is to remember it, so actively build a model and sort for patterns.
- Make associations: relate new information to what you heard before.
- Make use of imagery and all your senses. Make your model with coloured pictures, movement, surround-sound, smell, taste and feel.
- Organise the information, e.g. place symbols in space and events in sequence. Build your model of their information around them, not around yourself.
- Think about the logic and the implications of what you know. So if the client says she likes to 'see a long way', why is she considering buying a basement flat?

Remembering by using external aids:

- Write down the client's first words and key words/phrases.
- Highlight/star/underline information you would like to return to later.
- Mindmap—e.g. put desired outcome in the middle of the sheet. Construct 'branches' fanning out from it, with one branch for each symbol. Add 'twigs' to the branch to capture attributes, location, etc.

- Ask the client to map during the session and describe the map to you. Use what they say to catch and write down any key words you had forgotten. Receiving information via more than one sense helps you remember, so having both auditory and visual information means you are likely to remember more afterwards, even without writing any notes.

- Draw diagrams or pictures of your model of their information during the session (be discreet about this: keep your diagram to yourself).

Activity: Experimenting with remembering strategies

Go through the bullet points above, marking off all those you have already used to help you remember what your client has said. Now choose an unmarked bullet and experiment with using it by facilitating a partner.

* * *

Are there some contexts where this could be a useful strategy to use? Might it be still more useful if you 'tweaked' it a bit? If so, try the tweaked version in a subsequent session.

Q: **What if my client gets upset during a Clean Language session? What should I do?**

A: Because metaphors matter so much to people, it's not uncommon for strong emotional reactions to occur during Clean Language sessions.

Remember we mentioned 'going for the good stuff' earlier in the book? As a beginner it's best to avoid using Clean to explore problems or unhappy experiences, as this can prove uncomfortable and less effective. Use Clean Language to ask the questions predominantly about the *positive* aspects of a person's experience, their hopes for the future and their metaphors for these. That way you're likely to find things moving forward, fast.

Follow this advice, and you will decrease the likelihood of a client getting upset.

However, if your client does become upset, the first rule is to remain calm, and Clean—don't rush to 'comfort' them. Experiencing strong emotions may be exactly what's best for this client at this time, so give them a few moments to do what they need to do. Then consider asking, "And what would you like to have happen now?", a question which will frequently shift the client's attention and change their state.

Q.   What should I do when my client answers my question with, "I don't know"?

A.   Most importantly, relax! It's perfectly normal for clients to be unable to answer some questions, and it's important not to give the impression to your client that you are fazed by their answer or that they have done something wrong by giving an honest answer.

Often if you just pause before responding to their 'don't know' they'll keep thinking and will then be able to provide an answer to the question. If not, then simply repeat back their words as normal before backtracking to some other aspect of the metaphor landscape which has been mentioned. For example, the facilitator could say, "And you don't know. And trees, and lake, and sky. And when sky, is there anything else about that sky?"

Some clients answer such a lot of questions with 'I don't know', that it can be regarded as a pattern. For example, Judy has at least three different kinds of situation in which "I don't know" will be her answer. Sometimes she uses it when she can't think of an answer, sometimes when she has lots of answers and can't decide which to give, and occasionally when she knows the answer but doesn't want to reveal it. In Judy's case, an *advanced* facilitator working with her might choose to direct her attention to "I don't know" in the same way as any other client words, by asking a question about it. "And what kind of don't know is *that* don't know?" or "Is there anything else about *that* don't know?" would both be reasonable questions to ask.

But for beginners, the best way forward is simply to ask a Clean Language question about something else the client has mentioned.

Q. **When my client refers to himself as 'I', and I want to repeat his words back to him, should I use 'I' or 'you'?**

A. The answer is, 'It depends!'

Most often, using 'you' sounds more natural and normal to the client. "And you want to run faster. And when you run faster, what kind of faster is that faster?"

But there's an exception: when you want to ask your question about the 'I', you must repeat back 'I' rather than 'you' for your question to have the best chance of making sense. "And what kind of I is that I that wants to run faster?"

Q: **You mentioned Specialised Questions. What are these, and how should they be used?**

A: Many Clean facilitators use only the basic Clean Language questions. Sometimes, though, David Grove's Specialised Questions can be handy. They are:

Attributes

- *(And) does X have a size or a shape?*
- *(And) how many X's could there be?*
- *(And) how old could X be?*
- *(And) what could X be wearing?*

Location

- *(And) how far is [symbol's address]?*
- *(And) in which direction is/does [symbol's movement]?*
- *(And) is X (on the) inside or outside?*
- *(And) where is X [perceiving word, e.g. 'seeing'] that from?*
- *(And) where are you going when you go there?*
- *(And) where are you drawn to?*

Relationships

- *(And) is X the same or different as/to Y?*
- *(And) what's between X and Y?*

Intention

- *(And) would Y like [intention of X]?*
- *(And) would X be interested in going to Y?*

Time and sequence

- *(And) what's happening now?*
- *(And) what just happened?*
- *(And) what kind of X was that X before it was [attribute of X]?*

Source

- *(And) what determines whether X or Y?*

Knowing

- *(And) how do/will you know?*

These questions are to be used sparingly, and then only in ways that are consistent with the logic of the client's information. So if the client has mentioned having a child-like part of themselves it would be consistent with the information to ask, "And how old could that child be?" and/or "And what could that child be wearing?"

The question *"And how do you know?"* is valuable for establishing what criteria the client is using when they mention a concept. For example, if a client says, "Only then will I be happy again" you can ask, "And when you're happy again, how will you know you're happy?" This helps the client to attend to their embodied sense of 'happy' and invites them to respond with sensory or metaphoric information. Then you can ask more Developing Questions to help them self-model that state. This will likely result in easier accessing of that state in other contexts.

Some of the questions have 'you' as part of the question, and these are often used as an 'entry' into the client's metaphor landscape or into an as-yet-unexplored part of their landscape.

Activity: Using the Specialised Questions

Once you know the basic questions, you can start to use the Specialised ones. Read through the questions above and choose one or two that you think will be particularly useful. Write them on a piece of paper and put them where you'll see them often.

Make a point of using the questions when appropriate until you have mastered them. Then choose one or two more.

It is best to have memorised the basic questions first so that you can use them fluently.

Chapter 14
Where Else Can Clean Be Used?

*"Just remember: people tend to resist that which is forced upon them.
People tend to support that which they help to create"*
—Vince Pfaff

Because it works, Clean is catching on!

It may have started in the world of psychotherapy, but that was just
the beginning.

At the time of writing, we know of it being used in:

- Coaching
- Research
- Sales
- Recruitment
- Education
- Training
- Management
- Conflict resolution
- The creative arts
- Computing
- Spiritual development
- Government
- Healthcare
- Law enforcement
- Parenting
- and many other fields.

What needs to happen for you to use Clean every day?

Using Clean in conversation

Clean Language can be valuable in ordinary conversations, as well
as in more formal one-to-one settings. And ordinary conversations

are a great place to practise, not least because we have so many of them.

Activity: Clean Language questions in conversation

Each morning, select just one Clean Language question and resolve to use it in conversation at least three times during the day. Soon, you'll be amazed how easily the questions slide off your tongue.

Once you are confidently using Clean Language questions in conversation, you'll be able to slip almost invisibly from 'conversational' to 'full-syntax' Clean Language whenever you choose to.

Remember to check whether your intention is Clean. It's possible to be manipulative even with Clean Language. Do you have permission to work on a change topic with someone? Is it possible you're trying to 'fix' or to 'rescue' them—and if so, where does the urge to do so come from? If in doubt, always ask permission or don't pursue the topic.

There are a variety of possible ways to make Clean Language questions more conversational:

- Speak naturally and at a normal speed, without special emphasis.
- Keep it simple—only repeat occasional key words or phrases. In other words, use little or no syntax.
- Use pronouns such as 'that' and 'it' to represent their words in your question.
- Use more nodding and eye contact than usual to indicate you are really listening.
- Add 'musing' phrases to your questions such as "I wonder".
- Mingle Clean Language questions with other questions.
- Notice and use the person's metaphors as they naturally crop up, rather than asking "That's like what?"

Beginners sometimes assume that conversational Clean Language avoids going into a person's metaphoric landscape. They're often surprised to find this is not so. Metaphors are so much a part of how people think that they may barely notice when you ask questions using them. For example, many business managers use sporting metaphors continually, "We're all on the same side," "We want  to thrash the opposition," "Kick-off time," "Close of play," and so on. You can ask, "What kind of side is the side we're all on?" or "What would you like to have happen at close of play?" and expect that the speaker will—perhaps after some thought—have an answer to the question.

It often happens that after a Clean Language conversation, the client says that they had to think hard to answer the questions, that they found the conversation interesting and that it generated a different class of information from the norm.

Example conversational transcript: Holiday preparations

Speaker: I'm thinking about the next three days, getting everything sorted out before going on holiday. There's so much to do!

Questioner: Mmm, I see. What would you like to have happen?

Speaker: Be focused, so the crucial things get done and I can have a relaxed week on holiday.

Questioner: What kind of focused is that?

Speaker: Making distinctions ongoingly between what is crucial and what isn't.

Questioner: Anything else about those distinctions?

Speaker: They've got to keep happening. They're the kind of distinctions that happen when one's on the brink of leaving but I am wanting to make these distinctions before the very last minute, in the days before.

Questioner: And is there anything else about that?

Speaker: In that last-minute state it's easy to do. It's not usually very easy for me to do at other times.

Questioner: I see. What kind of state is a last-minute state?

Speaker: Acceptance that things can't be as good as I would like them to be.

Questioner: Anything else about that?

Speaker: It sounds funny, but I have to care less.

Questioner: I wonder, where could that come from?

Speaker: From knowing that there is no choice.

Questioner: Anything else about knowing?

Speaker: Kind of letting go.

Questioner: Oh! What kind of letting go is that?

Speaker: It's weird but to do that letting go I need a tight rein on my attention.

Questioner: And is there anything else about all that?

Speaker: I'm interested that I want 'letting go' and 'tight rein'. Usually my attention is on doing all the things as well as I can, and my attention then is not on me. Now the thing that I want done well, is me. That's what I want to hang onto so that when I leave, things are done adequately and the holiday can happen. I need to let go of the 'nice-to-haves' so my time gets spent just on the crucial bits of work.

Questioner: And what's happening right now?

Speaker:	I notice it's 5.31pm, which is an unusual thing for me to know. And I'm also interested in 'hanging on' and 'letting go'. I haven't thought about it like this before.
Questioner:	And then what happens?
Speaker:	I know what the time is. That's me 'hanging on' to my attention. What I'm doing now involves 'letting go' of a degree of the fascination that would normally be there to explore hanging on and letting go.
Questioner:	And what would you like now?
Speaker:	I'd like to leave it there and use what I know to get some crucial things done. Thanks!

Clean, Cleanish and content

In the real world, no interaction between two people can ever be completely Clean, but the addition of a Clean intention and some Clean Language questions can result in significant and valuable conversations.

Any particular interaction might be Clean, Cleanish or 'not Clean', depending on the facilitator's intention and on the amount of content (such as ideas, metaphors, information, instructions or advice) introduced by the facilitator. Clean Language questions will help you stay at the Clean Language end of the spectrum, but they aren't a guarantee. Ask a Clean question about something the other person has said and use a sarcastic tone of voice, or roll your eyes, and the result won't be at all Clean.

The 'Cleanness' of an interaction will also depend on your point of view. A well-facilitated Clean Language session involves the facilitator, not the client, behaving Cleanly while the client is *encouraged* to introduce their own content. So it is Clean from the facilitator's point of view, not from the client's.

You can't have a Clean Language conversation in which both people are perfectly Clean—some content needs to come from somebody. So in Clean Language conversations, for example when a manager meets with a member of her staff, or two friends get together, the roles of speaker and questioner are blurred, or may alternate over time. It's possible that one person asks most of the questions and stays largely Clean while the other is mostly in the speaker role. For example, it could be that the speaker wants help to understand their own behaviour, to make a change, or that the questioner wants to understand the speaker's perspective or find out how they do something expertly, either for their interest or in order to pass it on to others. On the other hand, the conversation could be a more 'normal' one with lots of give and take, in which the two people swap roles, each having a chance to add their input and each staying Clean while exploring their partner's 'stuff'.

Clean facilitators working in business settings often structure their conversations by alternating the delivery of their own content with the asking of Clean Language questions. This allows them to provide information and guidance (which is often what is expected of them in their business roles) while providing others with space and time to do their own thinking.

For example, a trainer hired to teach a specific skill would normally set a frame for the event, explaining what participants could expect and what was expected of them. He might set out his credentials and the basic principles of the new skill (content delivery) before using Clean Language questions to find out how his students intended to use what they learned. He could then provide an activity involving Clean Language questions so that they could each develop their own unique metaphorical image of themselves using their new skill, which would enable him to fine-tune his presentation of the next piece of content… and so on.

Once you have mastered the full set of Clean Language questions, you might also choose to extend your range to include 'Cleanish' questions, such as:

- What's that like?
- What would it be like if it was how you want it to be?
- When you *don't* want to be (or do) X, what *do* you want to be (or do)?
- What might have to happen?

These may be less effective than the standard Clean Language questions, but they can be useful in situations where you don't want to use phrasing that could seem unusual to the person with whom you're speaking.

You can also devise your own questions. As long as they fit with the logic of the client's landscape, and draw minimal attention to yourself, they count as 'Cleanish'. For example, your client might describe a landscape in which there are four cars: one is red, one blue and one green. It would then be Cleanish to ask, "And does the fourth car have a colour?"

Or when speaking to a manager who uses a team sport metaphor for his work, it would be Cleanish to ask, "What's the score?" or "Are you winning?"

Bear in mind that when you decide whether or not to be Clean, you need to be aware of your own goals and responsibilities, and to know why you choose to use Clean Language questions—or not. Perhaps you want to get to the nub of the issue quickly, while ensuring that everyone's experience is seen to be respected: that would be a good reason to use Clean Language questions. On the other hand, it may be that in that context it is respectful to show your own hand, too—and while this introduces content, which as we've pointed out is not Clean, there are Cleaner and less Clean ways of doing so. The Cleanest way to do that is by honestly, openly owning your own opinions and intentions.

Example transcript: Rodents.com

Developer:	(*Not Clean*) OK, you've drawn up the marketing plan, and building a website is the next step. (*Clean*) And now, what would you like to have happen?
Client:	I want my new website to attract millions of customers.
Developer:	(*Clean*) Millions of customers. What kind of customers?

Client:	People who are enthusiastic about keeping rodents as pets. So, young people, mainly, but some adults. The real enthusiasts and the people just getting started.
Developer:	(*Clean*) People who are enthusiastic about keeping rodents as pets. And you want to attract millions of customers to your website. And what kind of website?
Client:	Like Google! I want it so you can't miss it.
Developer:	(*Adding content*) Google is great, I use it all the time. But I think we might be working on a slightly different scale. In 2006, Google spent more than £800 million on persuading people to go to their site. I can build you something great, but I can't compete with Google. (*Clean*) And when all of that, what would you like to have happen?
Client:	Well, I didn't really mean like Google, that would be silly. But I'd like the site to be a hub for people who know about and love rodents …

A Clean Conversation structure

The following structure can be used for any Clean Conversation. It is especially useful at work, where the conversation is held with the intention of agreeing a way forward to the next stage of a project.

A Clean Conversation Structure

Set frame | Outline content and intended outcome of conversation

Starting question | And what would you like to have happen [with this frame in mind]?

Cleanly develop their response

Iterative loop

Reset frame | Recap developed response, restate frame, add relevant input

Starting question | And what would you like to have happen now [with this frame in mind]?
Or: And how is that for you?
Or: Can you work with that?

Closing | Summarise what has been discussed and what actions have been agreed

Take action

Based on work by Annemiek van Helsdingen, Wendy Nieuwland, Stefan Ouboter and others

Example transcript: *The performance review*

Manager: (*Sets frame*) As you know, we are here to review your performance and make plans for your development in the next year, given the current financial climate. With this in mind, what would you like to have happen?

Employee: Well let's start by discussing that unfortunate mistake I made. I want to get it out of the way, and then we can move on to discussing next year's plan.

Manager: OK, you'd like to discuss that mistake. Is there anything else about it? (*Cleanly develops response*)

Employee: Well, you know the circumstances. I was under pressure and I made an honest mistake.

Manager: So where could the mistake have come from? (*Cleanly develops response*)

Employee: Well, from being under pressure, obviously. I suppose my concentration slipped and somehow I misunderstood what was wanted. But you know I don't normally make mistakes like that.

Manager: What happened just before you made the mistake? (*Cleanly develops response*)

Employee: I was in a hurry, I'll admit that. I was trying to get all Julie's work done as well as my own. What I didn't do, that I normally would have done, was check back with the originator before sending the order out.

Manager: And what would you like to have happen in future? (*Cleanly develops response*)

Employee: Well, ideally, I'd like full cover for Julie's absence. But given that the business isn't prepared to do that, might it be possible to borrow John for two days a week, just to shift the backlog?

Manager: Well, as you know, that isn't something I can decide. But I'll certainly investigate it. After all, John's department owes us a favour! (*Adds his input*) And is there anything else that needs to happen in relation to the mistake?

Employee: I need to learn from it and not cut corners in the future, no matter how much pressure is going on.

Manager: OK, so it was a misunderstanding, an honest mistake, you were under pressure and you still are. I know you are aware of the effects your mistake had, and that you will learn from it and not cut corners in future. I'll check with John's department to see if he can be spared a couple of days a week. So, that's out of the way, what would you like to have happen now? (*Summarises conversation and actions so far, then moves on*)

Employee produces a document detailing his achievements and the conversation continues …

Using Clean with groups

Working with groups is a deep and rich topic—and an area in which Clean Language is developing quickly. Our comments here will be brief, just to whet your appetite and encourage further investigation.

❖ One way in which Clean Language is used with groups is in team alignment events, to help a team come up with a shared metaphor for working well together. The process might look something like this:

- Ask the team, "When our team is working really well together, it is like what?" Then invite each member of the team to draw their own individual metaphor picture to represent their personal answer.
- One by one, ask the members to show their pictures and describe their individual models to the others.

- Invite individuals to ask Clean Language questions about each person's picture. These questions help the model-owner to engage with their own values and beliefs, while also revealing them to the rest of the team. It also reveals the values, style and needs of the questioner.
- Using what is now known about all the various members' models and individual behaviours, ask the team to negotiate a shared metaphor for the team's mission. This collaborative process can mean revisiting individual models to elicit more information, and reviewing the team's desired outcome or managing potential conflicts. The aim is to agree a metaphor in which everyone has a stake.
- Finally, allow the team to work together to develop a representation of the shared metaphor, in the form of a larger picture or perhaps a physical model.[22]

This application demonstrates how basic Clean Language and the ideas which underpin it can be used with teams, and it's just one idea among many that are being explored and experimented with worldwide. What's best for a given situation depends upon the team and its desired outcome. What's clear is that Clean Language can profitably be used with groups in a huge variety of different situations.

---

[22] A version of this activity was originally devised by Caitlin Walker of Training Attention under the title 'Metaphors@Work'.

Chapter 15
Clean Success Stories

*"The marksman hits the target partly by pulling, partly by letting go.
The boatsman reaches the landing partly by pulling, partly by
letting go"*
—Egyptian proverb

Here is a selection of success stories which we hope will inspire you
to use Clean Language in your own life. Let us know how it goes by
emailing info@cleanchange.co.uk

Project leadership in the pharmaceutical industry

❖ A big company in the pharmaceutical industry was concerned
about the performance of some of their project leaders—the
individuals charged with testing new drugs and taking
them through to market. The process itself was highly regulated,
and although the procedure was being followed, there was
an extraordinary level of variation in the results delivered by
different individuals. What was happening?

A team of Clean Language consultants conducted a research
project to assess the differences between the top performers in
the role and their less-effective colleagues. By interviewing project leaders, their managers and members of their teams, they
were able to pinpoint specific areas of variability and make rec-
ommendations for how the company could improve performance.

Consultant Louise Oram explained, "It turned out that the
people who were most successful and highly regarded had
at least 15 years' experience in this kind of role, or were
programme managers who had come up through the ranks.

"We discovered that there were important differences between the thinking patterns of those who were good at the job and those who were not. Those who were good at the job knew what to look out for and had mental strategies for handling things that could go wrong, but they weren't necessarily aware of having these skills.

"The standard way of addressing this situation would have been a process review—but it was already clear they were following the process. By using Clean techniques we got a different class of information. This could be built into the individual development plans of the less-successful managers.

"People were saying to us, 'I didn't know I did that! Now I do know, I'll pay more attention to it.'

"Individual project leaders found that they now knew how to improve performance by changing their thinking strategies and their decision-making in the face of a mass of information."

As a result of the project, the company made specific changes to its selection procedure for the programme leader role, giving increased weight to the kinds of experience which had been found to be relevant. They also developed new career paths which encouraged experienced programme leaders to stay within the role.

Recruiting metaphorically

❖ Management Consultant Will Izzard has been using Clean in interviewing candidates for jobs. He said, "It really reveals a lot more about a person since they absolutely cannot have prepared answers for Clean Language questions.

"Not that I'm trying to catch them out or use 'trick questions'—my interviewing is sincere and authentic. Sometimes, Clean Language questions have revealed hidden talents. At other times, they've shown up incongruence in what a person says and this has sounded warning bells.

"For example, a chap I interviewed spoke about being keen in his role. I asked, 'What kind of keen?' 'Not keen like a puppy, but keen as in focused and concentrated on the task,' he said. Sounds great! Then, later on, he spoke about what he'd like to improve in himself, saying that sometimes he could lose concentration. 'Really?' I thought. So I asked, 'When lose concentration, what happens to keen, that is focused and concentrated on the task?'

"His answer had hinted to me that he'd probably like to be focused, but probably isn't in practice. I could then decide whether that would be a real problem in the work environment or if it was worth accepting and working on if he had other great skills.

"Then I co-interviewed a candidate with a rather sceptical colleague of mine. I didn't want to risk alienating my colleague with a very obvious-sounding technique, so I went for a very gentle approach. And here is the true power of Clean. Even with just a few 'What kind of ...?' questions and a couple of 'Is there a relationship ...' ones, my colleague was genuinely taken aback with the depth of information I'd managed to obtain from the candidate.

"She proceeded to tell lots of people in our company about how I somehow managed to 'magic' amazing and revealing information! Well of course I was very flattered, but far more impressed with the effect Clean had had on my colleague, who has now seen the benefit even without knowing what was happening."

Case study: Successful door-to-door sales and fundraising

❖ A company which employs a national force of fundraisers on behalf of several wildlife and conservation charities wanted to improve the results achieved by their new recruits so as to maximise revenue and reduce staff turnover.

A group of Clean Language consultants, including Judy, spent two days studying the sales approach taken by the company's top fundraisers. Using Clean principles in a combination of one-to-one interviews and group work, they distilled out ten factors which seemed to be crucial to success in this particular role, and reviewed the model with the top fundraisers and their managers. As the discussion continued, the metaphor of 'Wildlife Man' emerged as the ideal salesperson in this role—a friendly figure in a fleece jacket and stout walking shoes!

Judy said, "The company's entire sales force had been trained to use a short and highly-effective script on the doorstep. Given that the words said by each salesperson were almost identical, we needed to uncover what the top performers *did* as they said those words, and how they felt about what they were doing.

"As we started each interview with an open mind and a blank sheet of paper, the salespeople relaxed, felt they were being listened to and opened up to reveal unexpected details about the process they each used.

"At the same time, they discovered aspects of their performance that they had not noticed before. 'I didn't know I did that!' was a comment we heard frequently.

"For example, one salesman told himself 'It's showtime!' as he heard someone coming to answer the doorbell. This triggered a change in the way he held his body, and put a broad, welcoming smile on his face."

The company gained a new, very detailed understanding of the factors involved in the success of their top performers, and 'Wildlife Man' stepped into their new training procedures. As a bonus, they were able to update their recruitment criteria to improve the chances of long-term success.

A question of trust in the Dutch police force

❖ A department within the Dutch police force was obliged to act when a survey revealed that staff had a very low level of trust in their managers. After a round of meetings, poor communication was identified as a major issue.

How could the managers and team leaders change their communication style to help them build trust again? Over five half-day sessions, they were introduced to the principles of Clean Language and trained in Clean questioning and listening skills. As the impact of this work became clear, the project was extended and a group of staff received similar training.

Consultant Annemiek van Helsdingen (of consultancy Gewoon aan de Slag, based in Amersfoort, Holland) explained that she and Wendy Nieuwland chose to use Clean Language techniques because a lack of 'being heard' seemed to be at the core of the problem. People felt they were not being treated as individuals— managers and staff believed that everyone thought in the same way, and that whatever was true for one was true for all.

She said, "With Clean, you can't help but get to the specifics of a person's experience, thereby pinpointing what needs to change *for that person*. It's not the only tool for the situation, but it is a very effective one. The participants on the training were surprised to find out how hard it was to really listen, and how much energy was involved."

Afterwards, a further staff survey showed a clear shift in the right direction. Annemiek said, "The most senior manager has made a dramatic improvement in his communication style and skills, and it has been recognised by people. The same is true of a number of other managers, though not all.

"There are still some people saying things have not changed and never will change. But the majority are saying that things are heading in the right direction, but this mustn't be allowed to slip.

"Afterwards, the chief of the service said they had grown considerably as a management team. They communicate with each other very differently, have a much better eye for nuance (the difference that makes the difference), and they are much better equipped to deal with signals they get from within the organisation."

Training leaders as Clean motivators

❖ Weight Watchers Leaders learned how to use Clean Language principles to motivate members to lose weight. Each member has just a minute or two of the Leader's personal attention at the weekly meeting, so the organisation wanted to discover the fastest and most effective way to make a real difference.

Using Clean facilitation, a team including Marian Way, Phil Swallow and Wendy Sullivan devised a 'one-minute motivation' programme, which helps people focus on what they would like, and what steps they need to take to bring it about.

The programme is based on these questions:
– *And what would you like to have happen?*
– *What needs to happen for that to happen?*
– *And can you?*
– *And will you?*
(Note that the last of these questions is not one of the Clean Language questions).

This approach has been taught to 1,600 Weight Watchers Leaders in the UK and is being rolled out worldwide.

Cleaning up after conflict

❖ Martin Snoddon of the Conflict Trauma Resource Centre in Belfast is called in for post-conflict reconciliation work in some of the world's toughest hot-spots—not only in Northern Ireland, but also in the Balkans, in Israel/Palestine and elsewhere.

In Belfast, he used Clean Language to facilitate a meeting of angry residents, immediately after serious rioting in their area.

Martin said, "Initially, the group were stuck in an angry state, but as the anger abated I was able to move them from where they were to what they would like to have happen, and on to what needed to happen for that to happen.

"I worked with this group for six sessions that culminated with a viable strategic plan."

Martin has also worked with groups of ex-combatants, both military (British Army) and paramilitary (Republican and Loyalist). Clean Language questions helped to develop trust, so that they could explore more contentious issues safely.

The processes Martin has pioneered have led to reconciliation within communities and between communities—as well as helping individuals come to terms with their experiences. "Helping people to communicate their thoughts and feelings through the 'Clean' process so that they receive acknowledgement has been a tremendous asset," Martin said.

Fast team alignment

❖ A 'virtual team' of contact centre managers was experiencing problems. Their centres were widely spread geographically, but they needed to co-ordinate their efforts closely. Instead, the differences between centres were becoming more and more apparent, and friction was increasing.

The team came together for a day-long session facilitated by Wendy. First, the individual members of the team explored their own ideas about what their perfect working team would be like.

One man wanted the group to be like a Formula 1 pit crew team. Someone else wanted it to be like setting sail for distant shores. These metaphors have such different attributes and logic that it's not surprising that these two team members had been having a hard time working together. The other team members' symbols were all different and equally revealing.

Wendy said, "As each team member was asked about their symbol, there were nods and smiles as the team realised they had seen individuals 'living' their metaphors from day to day.

"For example, the 'Formula 1' person's meetings had no breaks for lunch or tea. People were expected to keep working and concentrating as long as there was work to do. He spoke fast, frequently losing team members who couldn't grasp the concepts flashing past at high speed."

The group then learned the skill of improving communication by using the individual metaphor of the team member they were talking to when they wanted to influence that colleague.

They also physically constructed a shared model for how they would like the team to be: a head with big ears for listening, lots of curly hair representing a zest for life, big eyes for taking in visual information and big, dangly earrings for an element of fun. As a reminder of the event, the model went 'on tour' around the team's different offices over the next year.

Communication within the team improved immediately, even before the day was over. As team members understood more about the thinking that generated a colleague's actions, it was simple for them to incorporate this into their communication and therefore to increase their influence with their colleagues. The regular conflicts and misunderstandings eased, resulting in improved communication across the contact centres, leading to improved customer service.

Getting clear in Whitehall

❖ Ken Smith, former head of Learning and Development at the Department of Culture, Media and Sport in Whitehall, uses his skills at work.

"One of my team had reached a time when he wanted to move on to something new, and wanted clarity on what this new thing might be. We had a first session using some NLP to elicit his values hierarchy, which gave him a set of criteria against which he could consider the job vacancies he found.

"Subsequently, he was uncertain about applying for a job he was interested in and asked if we could talk about this.

"I used a few Clean Language questions—e.g. what kind of challenge is that new challenge?—and he spent some time reflecting and processing, during which he apologised, saying, 'Sorry about all this rambling, I'm talking to myself really,' which of course told me the questions were working.

"He decided not to apply for that job and, perhaps with a little synchronicity, was approached by another manager a little while afterwards. He was invited to apply for a vacancy on her team, doing a job very much closer to what the values and Clean Language work suggested would be congruent for him. He got the job."

Developing a leadership team

❖ A leadership team within a global business faced big challenges as market conditions took a turn for the worse. There had been a number of personnel changes within the team, and the new people were struggling to integrate with established team members. The prevailing attitude tended to be 'I'm All Right Jack', with some departments favouring their own agendas at a cost to the business. Most of the team were feeling stressed and there was little laughter or banter. Management was acutely aware of its legal duty to alleviate stress in their employees.

Judy and Wendy worked on designing and delivering a multi-day event which combined team- and skill-building activities for the senior management team. It was the first time this team had spent significant time on team development.

The group learned to ask Clean Language questions of each other, and were astonished at the high quality of thinking, the number of insights and the ease with which they were able to disclose more than they had before. One team member admitted that he dreaded writing his part of the Board's monthly report, and realised that he could ask his colleagues for help with it—which he did. Two team members leapt at this, each offering a win-win exchange of skills. This led the team to realise that they could maximise their performance by agreeing not to judge each other as 'weak' for wanting help, but instead encouraging each other to say what they wanted or needed.

The group's enhanced questioning and listening skills helped to develop an atmosphere of openness. As a result they could discuss the new team members' experience of having to elbow their way in when faced with a united barrier of established team members 'ganging up' on them. Some solutions were suggested, and one or two implemented immediately by both new and established members, with established members asking for input from the new members and new members volunteering more.

When sharing their metaphors for how they wanted the team to be, they were surprised by how quickly they got to know what made each person—including themselves—'tick'. They discovered that they held divergent views about what an ideal team would be like, but in their new spirit of respecting each person's contribution they listened and asked Clean Language questions to understand the different metaphors. The metaphors naturally began to 'infect' each other and links between the various metaphors were spontaneously noticed, commented upon and developed.

During the event, the team developed an understanding of how to use Clean Language and metaphor in managing their staff from day to day, to inspire them and to open up a dialogue with the team as a whole or with individual team members. As well as eliciting the metaphors of their own staff, so as to understand and manage them better, the team members realised that they could elicit the metaphors of the departments that they worked alongside, and use those metaphors when interacting with those departments in order to frame activities in a way that would be accepted. For example, the marketing department was keen to improve how it worked with operations. The operations department said it wanted marketing to be like a temptress or a pied piper, beckoning them towards the pot of gold, in the same way marketing coaxed in customers. In response, the marketing department made an effort to present their plans in ways which were tempting to operations. In return operations volunteered some resources to trial new packaging which marketing had wanted for a long time.

The team were excited by the possibility of metaphor and started to use it as the principal way to communicate key messages within the organisation, which positively impacted on motivation. Metaphor began to be used to generate the vision for various teams on site, too.

The way in which Clean Language and metaphor could be used in non-work situations was clear to team members too, and they carried over their new skills to their home and social contexts to good effect.

When the team revisited their metaphors a few months later, a number of the individuals' metaphors had changed. Many clearly incorporated elements of other members' metaphors, making the metaphors more similar. This perhaps both reflected, and led to, a more aligned team.

They became a team that operated as a unit, more effective, more at ease with each other, and much noisier as they increasingly laughed and joked.

Modelling good clinical practice

❖ Wendy carried out a project in the National Health Service, exploring how clinicians, skilled in relating well to patients, do what they do. She found they had metaphors that unconsciously guided them, as each clinician spontaneously revealed their metaphor for relating to patients. One was a 'chameleon' (blending into the patient's world), another conducting a 'South East Asian business meeting' (conversation, doing business, further conversation).

After responding to a few Clean Language questions, their awareness was raised enough for them to use their metaphors to inform their working life. In one instance, this significantly raised the clinician's job satisfaction. In another, a doctor changed the way he taught practical work so junior doctors could build their rapport skills, too.

It's known that clinicians relating well to patients is very important to patients' outcomes, so it is hoped this work will become known well beyond those individuals directly involved.

Clean coaching goes down a storm with senior managers

❖ More than 250 UK senior managers at one of the 'big four' international accountancy firms, PricewaterhouseCoopers, have been introduced to Clean Language as a coaching tool during a benchmarking and development planning event. It has been going down very well.

Learning and development consultant Lorenza Clifford explained, "The two-day event is quite innovative in its design. The participants, who are senior managers, receive a lot of feedback during the event, so one of the key factors for success was to find a way to help managers to digest it and work with it, rather than be overwhelmed by it.

"Interspersed between assessment sessions there's a fairly chunky feedback session and then a co-coaching session to help them make sense of the feedback messages they've just received, and to put them together with previous feedback to see the themes that are emerging.

"We started out using GROW[23] for this co-coaching session. It's a well-known and useful coaching model, but it became clear that it was muddying the water in terms of the assessment process. We wanted something that wouldn't muddy the water, and for that Clean was great!

---

[23] GROW stands for Goal, current Reality, Options and Will. See John Whitmore, *Coaching for Performance*, 2002.

"Now, for co-coaching sessions, we set the participants up with a framework based on the Clean Language questions, and they can very quickly start to use it. It's useful because we're trying to encourage coaching and co-coaching generally, and giving them a different model that they can use quickly and easily with the managers who report to them, or with each other, makes a lot of sense.

"It's gone down a storm! Some people initially seem really sceptical when I describe the method and give an example, but they have a go. They often come out of the session saying, 'I couldn't see how it was going to work, but when I was on the other end of it, being coached, it was great! They just let me come up with my own stuff.' "

Chapter 16
Next Steps

"The most basic of all human needs is the need to understand and be understood. The best way to understand people is to listen to them"
—*Ralph Nichols*

Welcome to the end of the beginning!

And what would you like to have happen now?

Clean Language is an unusual way of thinking about the way people think. In this book we have offered a straightforward explanation which has allowed it to be put to work by insightful people in a whole variety of situations. We have only provided a brief introduction. There's a great deal more we could have included—this fast-moving field always has something new and exciting to offer.

If you'd like to take your interest further, here are some suggestions.

Keep practising

As you've worked through the exercises in this book, you've probably already enlisted the help of friends and colleagues as 'clients' to practise with. Now you've reached the end of the book, keep the practice going.

Remember that, as well as in face-to-face sessions, Clean Language can be used:

- on the phone
- via instant chat messaging on the internet
- in business meetings

- in casual conversations
- in 'coaching' conversations with children—or simply to hear about their day

and in many other ways. Using some of these opportunities each week will soon pay off in skills development.

If you are short of practice partners, you might try http://www.cleanforum.com

The site is also a good place to find fellow enthusiasts to discuss what you've learned from this book. As with all public forums, it may sometimes be worth taking what you are told with a pinch of salt!

Review transcripts

Many facilitators find it helpful to record and transcribe sessions (with the client's permission) for review. You can go through the transcript looking for:

1. Your questioning preferences:
   - Were there any Clean Language questions you didn't use?
   - Do you tend to ask about nouns, verbs or adjectives?
   - Do you ask most of your questions about their metaphor or about abstract information? (Generally it is easiest and most productive to work in metaphor.)
   - Do you ask questions about the client's problem by mistake?

2. Going along with the suggested order and proportion of questions in a session:
   - Do you have a tendency to ask for a metaphor of a metaphor (which can annoy or puzzle a client)?
   - Do you have the good habit of asking a significant number of location questions?
   - Do you hold off asking about necessary conditions for change until the metaphor is well developed?
   - Do you spend time on maturing changes in the client's landscape?

3. Kinds of information:
   - Look for any desired outcomes that the client mentioned. Did you spot them all during the session?
   - Find all the metaphors the client used.
   - Underline abstract language.
   - Look for any times when the client became focused on their problem, and you didn't notice they were not attending to their desired outcome.

4. Patterns of the client:
   - Can you find patterns in how the client communicates? For instance, they may give lots of unnecessary details, or may be hyper-aware of the facilitator's needs so that they don't easily put their attention on themselves.
   - Are there patterns in relation to their content? Always starting to answer a question with their attention on their problem, and then changing their perspective to consider their desired outcome, for example.
   - What patterns can you notice about their behaviour?
   - What words do they use frequently?

Read, listen and view

We recommend reading James Lawley and Penny Tompkins' book *Metaphors in Mind*, and watching their DVD *A Strange and Strong Sensation*. They also have an extensive library of articles about Clean Language which is available at http://www.clean language.co.uk

Other materials, including downloadable recordings and transcripts of other facilitators' sessions, are available from http://www.cleanchange.co.uk

Attend (or form) a practice group

One of the most inexpensive—and fun—ways to build your skills is to get together with other enthusiasts to practise. It is such an effective way to keep building skills that many of the most experienced Clean Language facilitators continue to attend such groups.

By working with multiple practice partners, you will be exposed to a more diverse range of metaphoric landscapes and ways of describing them; there will be different patterns and different styles of facilitation to enjoy.

By being facilitated using Clean Language, you will become more aware of your own patterns. As we have seen, this will help keep your facilitation Clean and flexible. And, of course, the regular bursts of being a client mean you benefit from ongoing personal development.

Face-to-face practice groups exist in various areas of the UK and elsewhere. There are also groups that 'meet' via the internet. To set up your own, all you need is two or more participants, an agreed date and time and a venue—real or virtual. Groups typically meet for 90 minutes or two hours, allowing time for introductions, setting up an activity, some work in pairs or threes (with an observer, facilitator and client) and sharing experiences and learnings.

The website http://www.cleanforum.com is a great place to look for details of existing groups, and to find possible members for new groups. You can also find details of practice group activities which have been used by others.

Attend a basic training

No book can ever compare to the experience of a training event, and attending basic training will make a huge difference to your Clean Language facilitation skills.

- The foundation skills of Clean Language facilitation will be brought more fully to life, presented in ways which appeal to all your senses.
- You'll have all the advantages that come from working informally with other enthusiasts, but in a more focused, directed context.
- You'll have a skilled trainer and a team of experienced assistants, all keen to offer support, give feedback and fine-tune your approach.

We'd be delighted to see you on a Clean Change Company training event: details are on our website http://www.cleanchange.co.uk

For training with other organisations you can find details at http://www.cleanlanguage.co.uk and www.cleanforum.co.uk

You may find that your trainer has a different take on the material from that described in this book. Please be aware that Clean is an unregulated field, with all that that entails.

Advanced Clean training

To use Clean Language in more challenging, specialised situations, such as with long-standing problems which have resisted multiple attempts at change, in personal development or in business, more advanced training will be valuable.

Some areas covered in our advanced trainings include:

- Penny Tompkins and James Lawley's Framework for Change and other Approaches to Change. The Framework includes 'PRO', a way to identify and redirect attention when the client isn't focused on their desired outcome. Exploring these models can provide you with greater flexibility to respond in the moment to new and unusual situations.
- Space: Some of the most exciting Clean developments involve working with space. With processes such as Clean Space, clients get a very different perspective on their 'stuff', and reaching a number of new insights in quick succession is commonplace.

- Scaling and thresholds: As you may already have discovered, symbols in metaphor landscapes are often strangely scaled, unusually large or small in relation to the client or each other. An understanding of the role of scale in human cognition can give your Clean Language facilitation a new edge.
- Binds and double-binds: Catch-22 situations can keep people and organisations 'stuck'. Modelling them Cleanly can provide new insights which get things moving forward.
- Self-delusion, self-denial and self-deception. These often-useful strategies can at times become problematic and can stop us from being able to formulate a desired outcome, prevent us from having access to that desired outcome landscape, block us from knowing what conditions need to be in place or how to achieve them, or stop us from making or maintaining changes in real life. Working Cleanly to enable a client to recognise their self-delusion may transform the situation.

Conclusion

Thank you for reading this book, and for allowing us to share our passion for Clean Language with you.

Wherever your journey takes you, enjoy it—and do let us know what happens next by emailing info@cleanchange.co.uk

Appendix 1
The Basic Clean Language Questions

Developing Questions

- *(And) what kind of X (is that X)?*
- *(And) is there anything else about X?*
- *(And) where is X? or (And) whereabouts is X?*
- *(And) is there a relationship between X and Y?*
- *(And) when X, what happens to Y?*
- *(And) that's X like what?*

Sequence and Source Questions

- *(And) then what happens? or (And) what happens next?*
- *(And) what happens just before X?*
- *(And) where could X come from?*

Intention Questions

- *(And) what would X like to have happen?*
- *(And) what needs to happen for X?*
- *(And) can X (happen)?*

Appendix 2
The Specialised Clean Language Questions

Attributes
- *(And) does X have a size or a shape?*
- *(And) how many X's could there be?*
- *(And) how old could X be?*
- *(And) what could X be wearing?*

Location
- *(And) how far is [symbol's address]?*
- *(And) in which direction is/does [symbol's movement]?*
- *(And) is X (on the) inside or outside?*
- *(And) where is X [perceiving word, e.g. 'seeing'] that from?*
- *(And) where are you going when you go there?*
- *(And) where are you drawn to?*

Relationships
- *(And) is X the same or different as/to Y?*
- *(And) what's between X and Y?*

Intention
- *(And) would Y like [intention of X]?*
- *(And) would X be interested in going to Y?*

Time and Sequence
- *(And) what's happening now?*
- *(And) what just happened?*
- *(And) what kind of X was that X before it was [attribute of X]?*

Source
- *(And) what determines whether X or Y?*

Knowing
- *(And) how do/will you know?*

References

Bandler, Richard and Grinder, John, *Reframing*, Real People Press, 1982

Dilts, Robert, Hallbom, Tim and Smith, Suzi, *Beliefs*, Metamorphous Press, 1990

Evans, Vyvyan and Green, Melanie, *Cognitive Linguistics: An Introduction*, Lawrence Erlbaum Associates, 2006

Fauconnier, Gilles and Turner, Mark, *Conceptual Blending and the Mind's Hidden Complexities*, Basic Books, 2002

Faulkner, Charles, *Metaphors of Identity* (Audio recording), Genesis II, 1991

Geary, James, *Geary's Guide to the World's Greatest Aphorists*, Bloomsbury US, 2007

Gibbs, Raymond W Jr., 'Categorization and metaphor understanding', *Psychological Review* 99(3): 572–577, 1992

Haidt, Jonathan, *The Happiness Hypothesis*, Arrow Books, 2007

Johnson, Mark, *The Body in the Mind*, University of Chicago Press, 1987

Kline, Nancy, *Time to Think: Listening to Ignite the Human Mind*, Cassell Illustrated, 1998

Kovecses, Zoltan, *Metaphor: A Practical Introduction*, Oxford University Press, 2002

Lakoff, George and Johnson, Mark, *Metaphors We Live By*, University of Chicago Press, 1980

Lakoff, George and Johnson, Mark, *Philosophy In The Flesh*, Basic Books, 1999

Lawley, James and Tompkins, Penny, *Metaphors in Mind: Transformation Through Symbolic Modelling*, Developing Company Press, 2000

Miller, Anne, *Metaphorically Selling*, Chiron Assoc. Inc., 2004

Morgan, Gareth, *Images of Organization*, Sage, 1997

Morgan, Gareth, *Imaginization*, Sage, 1993

Panzer, B. I. and Grove, David J., *Resolving Traumatic Memories*, Irvington, 1989

Pink, Daniel, *A Whole New Mind*, Riverhead Books, 2006

Pinker, Steven, *How the Mind Works*, Penguin, 1997

Pinker, Steven, *The Stuff of Thought*, Viking Penguin, 2007

Robertson, Ian, *Mind Sculpture*, Bantam Books, 2000

Tompkins, Penny and Lawley, James, *A Strange and Strong Sensation* (DVD), Developing Company Press, 2003

Turner, Mark, *Reading Minds*, Princeton University Press, 1993

Whitmore, John, *Coaching for Performance*, Nicholas Brearley, 2002

Williamson, Marianne, *A Return to Love*, Harper Collins, 1992

Wilson, Robert Anton, *Prometheus Rising*, New Falcon Publications, 1992

Zaltman, Gerald, *How Customers Think*, Harvard Business Press, 2003

Zaltman, Gerald and Zaltman, Lindsay, H., *Marketing Metaphoria*, Harvard Business Press, 2008

Index

Praise for Clean Language

Clean Language deserves to be a multi-purpose tool of choice in the kitbag of coach, facilitator and even salesperson; this excellent guide will show you how to use it effectively.

> Max Landsberg, Author of *The Tao of Coaching*, former Partner at McKinsey & Co, and Partner at Heidrick & Struggles

Clean Language is a simple questioning technique to get people to explore their own internal metaphors, understand them and motivate them to change, claim its proponents. It was developed by counselling psychologist David Grove. This book shows how it can be taken into conversations at home, school and work.

> Human Givens

Wendy Sullivan and Judy Rees have done a valuable service in bringing practical and accessible learning to Clean Language. Having been invited by the founder of 'Clean', David Grove to Auckland, NZ., I was exposed to his genius. Like others before me, most notably, authors Penny Tompkins and James Lawley (who made 'Clean Language accessible to others), I became increasingly hooked on David's thinking and methods. It is easy to understand why Sullivan and Rees became similarly addicted and why their journeys have brought them to offer us such a valuable book.

There is a gap between seeing and experiencing masterful facilitation using Clean Language and reading about it. A reader without this access must therefore trust that 'Clean' can and does deliver extraordinary awareness and positive change – and it does. The book must appeal to newcomers to 'Clean' and the thoughtful evolution of the text, rich in examples, explanations, re-iteration of key learnings and activities make it a delightful journey.

From a quality standpoint, Clean Language offers the prospect of a higher and more consistent level of practitioner professionalism than most alternative awareness and change-methodologies including coaching. These two factors, together with its impact and professional standard must ensure that the developmental journey of 'Clean' will continue wide and deep. Sullivan and Rees have contributed a worthy book to help that valuable journey on its way. I commend this book.

> Dr Angus McLeod, author of *Performance Coaching,*
> *Me Myself My Team, and Self-coaching Leadership*

Metaphors are woven so deeply and so commonly into the fabric of our spoken communication that we hardly notice how rich and patterned they are. Yet these metaphors carry within them the very strands of our deepest thoughts and feelings about the world and our relationship to it. If we follow the threads that our metaphors point us towards, if we take time to tease out and untangle their meaning and significance, then we discover a royal road to a deeper understanding of ourselves and others. The individual metaphors we each use offer the most extraordinary insights into our deepest and most hidden meaning-making processes; they reveal with extraordinary vividness and texture just how we unconsciously design and construct our 'reality.'

In their practical, hands-on, easy-to-read book, *Clean Language*, Wendy Sullivan and Judy Rees have done an exceptional job in showing just how to tease out and reveal the metaphors we live by and how to change, consolidate, develop, or transform them as we might wish. They reveal, in an easy-to-grasp, step-by-step approach, how working with, revealing, and consciously shaping, our metaphors can easily and effortlessly transform our lives.

In doing so they have taken the Clean Language and Clean Change ideas of David Grove, James Lawley, and Penny Tompkins, and created a powerful guide that makes this work both highly accessible and more mainstream. And it is written in a way that will benefit and attract both the beginner and the more advanced user.

I particularly appreciated the authors' generosity in sharing so much of the process, as well as their integrity and enthusiasm. The activities are well thought out and useful and the examples and case histories offer a clear indication of the many possible applications of Clean over a wide variety of contexts.

Above all, I was taken by the aikido of the process: the way Clean works with the inner energy and natural strategies of the client without force or effort; the artistry and skill of the facilitator is in simply staying clean and attentive to the client's world and outcomes.

The Clean Language process is powerful and artful precisely because it works with people the way they naturally are. It works because it recognises that each individual is a uniquely integrated system that is both deeply wise and elegantly self-organising rather than a collection of parts to be fixed. It works because it offers deep sustainable change, and because – ultimately - all our stories, and all our metaphors, come true.

Nick Owen, trainer, consultant, coach and author of *The Magic of Metaphor, More Magic of Metaphor* and *The Salmon of Knowledge*

Wendy Sullivan owns West London-based Clean Change Company. Go to **www.cleanchange.co.uk** to find out about:

- The world's most comprehensive training in Clean Language and Symbolic Modelling. You can start with a two-day introduction or dive into a two-week foundation course, and progress to advanced courses led by Wendy, together with Penny Tompkins and James Lawley.

- Clean Conference, which brings together Clean enthusiasts from all over the world.

- Clean Change Cards, which will help you learn and use the Clean Language questions.

- Audio and video recordings of Clean Language sessions and related materials.

- Coaching and therapy sessions using Clean Language.

Judy Rees applies Clean Language in business contexts, working with individuals and project teams to help them develop more effective communication skills, so that misunderstandings are reduced and effectiveness improved. Her background is in news journalism and in managing new media and other information technology projects, and her consulting work focuses primarily on these industries. **www.judyrees.co.uk**